BIG BEND GUIDE

Top 10 Travel Tips
Top 10 Hikes
& Top Itineraries for the Casual Visitor

By Allan C. Kimball

3RD EDITION

The Great Texas Line Press

Fort Worth, Texas

Copyright © 1996, 2008, 2016 by Allan C. Kimball
All rights reserved.
No portion of this book may be reproduced in any form without written
permission of the publisher.

Cover photos by Lawerence Parent
Inside photos by Allan C. Kimball
Illustrations by Marcus McMullin
Book design by Jeff Stanton

For bulks sales and wholesale inquiries, contact:
Great Texas Line Press
Post Office Box 11105
Fort Worth, Texas 76110

greattexas@hotmail.com
www.greattexasline.com
Tel. (800)73TEXAS

All the information in this guide was correct when it went to press. As with
any guide, however, some information changes. The author's recommendations expressed in this book are the opinions of the author only, and any
omission of any entity is not meant as disparaging in any way. The publisher and author disclaim any liability for any loss or damage or problems
caused by errors, omissions, or misleading information in this guide.

Thanks to Erin & Brian
and especially Madonna

"God chooses your relatives. Thank God you can choose your friends."
— English proverb

TABLE OF CONTENTS

Author's Note

When I was eight years old, playing in my grandfather's attic, I discovered a chest full of wonders. It yielded an old khaki cavalry uniform and campaign hat, a well-worn Colt .45 automatic in a cracked leather military holster, rolls of U.S. $10 gold pieces, a small canvas bag of Mexican coins, dozens of dog-eared dime novels, a couple of hand-colored postcards with Western themes, and hundreds of faded photographs of a strange place full of adobe structures and desolate vistas and bodies hanging from poles in village courtyards.

I asked him about the pictures. Over a number of conversations, my grandfather told me about chasing the revolutionary leader Pancho Villa, to him a Mexican bandit general, all over the Chihuahuan Desert while headquartered at posts in southwest Texas. He told me about dry deserts and painful plants and lush oases and rugged mountains and skies that went on forever.

When he died in 1969, I was determined to see the places he had told me about, and so later that year I drove to the Big Bend. It was a very empty place then; even the national park drew few visitors. His old cavalry posts at Lajitas and Castolon were in ruins.

Something kept drawing me back. Over the years, I watched the area grow, often cringing as roads were widened and raised by progress. Motels were built, shacks began to dot the hills and the desert. Seldom Seen Slim and Suitcase Sally came and went, along with many friends.

I discovered a photo in W.D. Smither's fine book, *Chronicles of the Big Bend*, which showed Sgt. William Henry "Bud" Kimball astride a horse behind the famous Capt. Leonard Matlack. In later readings, I learned that my grandfather was likely one of two men who confronted a mountain lion in the Chisos Mountains while on a scouting trip and named the place Panther Peak, at the foot of which the national park headquarters now stands.

One evening in the middle 1970s, I was staying at the Cavalry Post

Motel in Lajitas, built on the ruins of Sgt. Kimball's old post, and walked outside from my room to get a Coke from a vending machine at the end of the wing. The sky was dark and more full of stars than you can imagine. I could hear a goatherd moving his charges in the distance, a bell or two tinkling on the wind in accompaniment to his almost whispered Spanish. My cowboy boots clunked against the boardwalk, perhaps not unlike the sound my grandfather's boots made so many decades ago, and I fell in love with Big Bend right there.

I hope you come to love Big Bend as much as I do.

You go south from Ft. Davis
until you come to the place
where rainbows wait for rain,
and the river is kept in a stone box,
and water runs uphill.
And the mountains float in the air,
except at night when they go away to play
with other mountains
— Anonymous Mexican vaquero

INTRODUCTION

You are about to embark on a unique adventure.

These pages should be of great help to you, whether you're planning a trip into one of our nation's most scenic and untamed areas or whether you're already in the Big Bend country of Texas.

This is an informal guide for casual travelers to Big Bend National Park, Big Bend Ranch State Park, and the surrounding area. It's for those who want to see and experience all they can of this singular countryside in a limited time, or on a limited budget, or with limited skills or interests. It's a guide for those who will travel about almost exclusively in a motor vehicle, and for those who venture off mostly on day hikes. It is especially a guide for those visiting Big Bend for the first time.

This book is meant neither to be an in-depth guide to survival in the Chihuahuan Desert nor a guide for backpacking several days into the beautiful, treacherous areas therein. It's not a detailed history of the region. It's not a field guide to animals or plants or rocks or birds. And it's not an embellished map to the national or state parks in Big Bend. Those books have already been written (see the *Recommended Reading* section at the back of this guide).

Big Bend Guide is aimed at providing the best advice on some of the area's key sites and activities. It's full of my opinions, which may differ from those of others, and no doubt some folks will be glad to argue a point or two. But my recommendations are based on decades of travel in the Big Bend and as well as on time spent on my land in Lajitas and Terlingua.

The book is in three parts.

The first details what you will need to make your stay in the Big Bend a comfortable, enjoyable, and safe one. The most common mistake by casual visitors is in simply not taking the area seriously enough. Enough roads crisscross Big Bend to make most of the areas easily accessible. Yet it remains one of the most primitive locations in the continental United States with extremes of terrain and weather that *do* take lives. Don't let this warning alarm you, however. Big Bend is also one of the best areas in the country should you want to experience nature at its purest, to surround yourself with history, to see scenic vistas that will take your breath away. It can make your life miserable, too. If you understand what sort of place Big Bend is, and what sort of precautions and clothing and footwear to take, you will return home with happy memories instead of a broken car, a splitting headache, a sore back and blisters.

The second part is a list of the best day hikes. Unless restricted by health reasons, to visit Big Bend and not get out on a trail is to miss a significant part of the experience. Not to worry, though, for the area is renowned for having hikes that range from the very easy to the very strenuous. Take your pick, arm yourself with water, proper clothing, and a camera, and off you go.

The third part is a series of suggested itineraries for visiting the Big Bend area, from Boquillas Canyon in the east to the Solitario in the west to Fort Davis in the north. The itineraries are of two, five and ten days, along with other options. In each are suggestions on what to do and see — and how to get there — on each day to get the most out of your stay.

All the recommended stops are rated with stars, the more the better:

★★★★ = You must see this place.

★★★ = Try hard to see this place.

★★ = See this place if you can.

★ = If you've got the time, check this place out.

Big Bend National Park is the reason most people visit the area the first time, but you'll discover many other things to do and see in the surrounding area including Big Bend Ranch State Park, Davis Mountains State Park, Fort Davis National Historic Park, Fort Leaton State Historic Site, McDonald Observatory, Hallie's Hall of Fame, Stillwell Canyon, the cities of Alpine, Fort Davis, Marathon, Marfa, Ojinaga, and Presidio, and along all the roads that connect them. To see everything of interest here would take a serious visitor a lifetime.

To aid you in planning an individual and varied trip schedule, this book also includes some of those options in areas away from Big Bend National Park.

Enjoy your visit.

PART ONE
TOP 10 TRAVEL TIPS

Everything in the desert either pricks, sticks or stings.
— Apache saying

Welcome to the Big Bend

The lizard-like stillness in the Big Bend is a powerful intoxicant.

This is one of the few places left in the United States virtually unchanged for centuries. What you see, hear, smell, feel, and taste here are the same as encountered by prehistoric peoples, as Apache and Comanche Indians, as invading Spaniards, as goatherds and cowboys, as miners, as settlers and smugglers did.

This is nature, painted raw and large. You will feel exhilaratingly lonely sitting on a desert mesa, walking through the Chisos Mountains, or floating down the Río Grande. The scant evidence of humans you will see seems frail and very temporary.

The abandoned mines you see here were mostly for cinnabar, the stuff of quicksilver. You will still find chunks of it scattered over the hills, looking like rusted rocks. Silver was mined here, too, until it got more expensive to dig it up than it was worth.

Woody Guthrie even wrote about finding a rich vein of gold on what is now the national park, but no one else has ever found that. Pioneers who overgrazed and other factors led to the decline of native grasses. Homesteaders and entrepreneurs tried to carve out places for themselves in this inhospitable countryside and most of them failed.

Looking across the Sierra Quemada — the Burned Mountains — from the South Rim of the Chisos, you see Mexican summits nearly lost in the mists of miles; you see eagles soaring below you. It takes your breath away.

Here the Río Grande makes its dramatic detour, its big bend, along the Texas border, dipping sharply south at Lajitas to rise again northward at Boquillas. Here, Tex meets Mex in a blend of language, food, culture and heritage unknown anywhere else in the country. This is the place outsiders usually picture when they hear the word "Texas." This is the place the Spanish conquistadores abandoned as being too hot, too desolate, too uninhabitable — el despoblado.

Big Bend is distinctive in that it is made up of three diverse ecosystems: mountains, desert, river.

The Chisos Mountains lurch from the Chihuahuan Desert like a giant ship at sea. The Chisos rise as high as 7,825 feet on Emory Peak, one of the highest mountains in Texas, creating a temperate environment in the midst of the arid desert. About a mile high, the Chisos Basin is the center of activity in the Big Bend National Park. Surrounded by looming peaks are motel rooms and cabins and campgrounds, a general store, an amphitheater where rangers give daily talks and demonstrations, picnic areas and a restaurant offering a majestic view of the desert far away and far below.

About 95 percent of the park is Chihuahuan Desert, a desert that can defy stereotype and be remarkably green. The blooms here in early spring are stunning, especially the giant dagger yuccas that tower over you. The pine and juniper in the high Chisos are familiar, but even the names of the desert flora excite a traveler's imagination: acacia, agave, candelilla, catclaw, cenizo, chamisa, cholla, creosote, guayacan, leatherstem, lechuguilla, mesquite, nolina, ocotillo, sotol, tasajillo, and yucca. And strawberry, eagle claw, rainbow and prickly pear cactuses.

The Río Grande creates a ribbon of oasis across the desert. It's almost tropical. Standing amid river cane, tropical ferns and cottonwood trees at the mouth of Santa Elena Canyon, where Terlingua Creek flows into the Río Grande, it's easy to picture the pterosaurs that once spread their 50-foot wingspans and glided from these very cliffs. They were the largest animal — bird, reptile, or mammal — ever to take flight.

Big Bend National Park, established in 1944, sprawls over an area larger

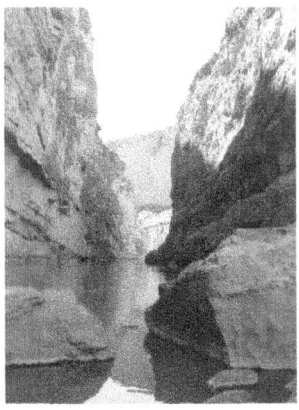

than Rhode Island — more than 800,000 acres with 300 miles of paved roads, another 150+ miles of unpaved roads and more than 150 miles of hiking trails.

The idea for a national park began with *Fort Worth Star-Telegram* publisher Amon Carter, Hot Springs resort owner J.O. Langford, and Brewster County sheriff and later state legislator E.E. Townsend in the early 1900s, but it wasn't until Townsend was elected to the Legislature that their ideas began to roll toward reality.

They began buying up property to donate for the park, but the National Park Service wasn't interested, so they convinced Texas to create a state park. First called Texas Canyons State Park, then Big Bend State Park. The trio's ultimate goal was to have *two* national parks, one in the U.S. and an adjacent park in Mexico, creating one huge international peace park.

The federal government got involved early, with the Civilian Conservation Corps creating roads, hiking trails, and cabins in the Chisos Mountains that are still in use today.

More land was bought by the state—not an easy thing after the Great Depression sapped the economy and with the nation dealing with World War II. Finally, on June 12, 1944, the state transferred the park to the National Park Service.

Efforts to establish the park's Mexican counterpart failed repeatedly over the decades until 1994 when Mexico created the Maderas del Carmen Protected Natural Area in the state of Coahuila and Cañon de Santa Elena Protected Area of Flora and Fauna in the state of Chihuahua, both directly across from Big Bend National Park. Ironically, before any infrastructure could be completed on the Mexican preserves, the U.S. closed all the unofficial border crossings along the Río Grande in May 2002 in the wake of the events of 9/11, making easy access to the great ecological paradise straddling the river impossible. Perhaps the original dream of an international park will one day be realized.

Big Bend National Park is a remarkably diverse region. Researchers have identified more than 1,000 species of plants, 434 species of birds, 75 species of mammals, 55 species of reptiles, and 34 species of fish. In 1976, the United Nations recognized the unique value of Big Bend and declared the area an International Biosphere Reserve.

Big Bend Ranch State Park was established in 1988 and is only recently becoming more accessible to visitors. The park is also quite large with more than 300,000 acres—when it was acquired it effectively doubled the acreage in the Texas State Park system. And it's even more primitive than the national park.

The ranch the park is named for was started by brothers Gallie, Gus, and Woodworth Bogel when they consolidated several small cattle and goat ranching operations during the 1910s. A severe drought in the 1930s, from which much former ranch land in the Big Bend has yet to recover, forced the Bogels into bankruptcy and the ranch was purchased by another set of brothers, Mannie and Edwin Fowlkes. Ownership then changed hands several times until it was bought by a company owned by R. O. Anderson and Walter Mischer (who created the Lajitas Resort). They sold it to the state for the park in 1988.

Because the ranch had so many environmentally sensitive areas, it was first designated as a state natural area and didn't officially allow public visitation into the heart of the park until 1991. The designation was changed to a state park and plans were made over the next decade to make the area more accessible. That plan is only now being implemented, and visitors will discover a true gem in the raw.

But whether you're visiting the national park, the state park, or any of the areas around them, you don't go to Big Bend on a Saturday afternoon whim. Big Bend is way off the beaten path and you're going to need a vehicle to see it. Buses and trains, and sometimes, small planes, run to Alpine, 100 miles to the north, while the nearest major airport with scheduled flights is 250 miles away in Midland. (See the *Traveling* section for more details.)

The magic begins once your vehicle heads south from either Interstate 10 or U.S. Highway 90 as the scrub flatlands give way to looming mesas and, eventually, desert fauna and the ghostly mountains in the distance.

Yours can be a trip to remember. You may see the mysterious Marfa Lights, the incredible range of colors locked in rock at a desert tinaja, the ruins of an old mine or ranch or wax factory, Del Carmen whitetail deer and javelina from your front porch, ocotillo afire in orange blossoms, balanced rocks and strange hoo-doos, a sunset blazing through the Window in the Basin of the Chisos.

People have spent a lifetime here and not seen all there is to see. Better get started.

10. TRAVELING

Most people travel to Big Bend by car. One reason is that the distances between places are so vast you need your own transportation to get around at all. The other reason is that few other options exist. One way to judge just how far off the beaten path you are is to consider that when you are along the Río Grande in Big Bend you are more than 160 miles from the nearest Wal-Mart.

✔ By Air

Alpine has a municipal airport, and over the years small companies have run commercial flights in. The demand is so small, however, that those routes have come and gone with the same regularity as restaurants between Terlingua and Study Butte. You can always fly in on a private plane, but remember that getting to Alpine still means you're 100 miles and more away from any of the park areas. Rental cars are usually available.

Terlingua Ranch has an airstrip that will accommodate small private planes, and a smaller, informal strip is located near the Terlingua Store. The Lajitas Resort has a much larger airstrip that can handle small jets. If you make arrangements in advance you can rent cars from the auto repair shop in Study Butte.

✔ By Train

Amtrak's Sunset Limited chugs into Alpine a couple of times each week traveling between Los Angeles and New Orleans and all points in between, and trains can be a great way to travel since you can relax and watch the scenery or read or nap. Schedules change, so check with your travel agent. Once in Alpine, though, you face the same problems as if you flew in. You'll need a car to go anywhere.

✔ By Car

Gas up in Alpine or Marfa, and once you're south of those cities you would be wise to top off your tank every time you see a gas station because you won't see many gas stations out here (although there are more than there were just a few years ago). Prices are higher than in the rest of the state.

Distances are vast. For example, if you're camping at Río Grande Village in the national park and decide you want to visit Ojinaga, across from Presidio, you'll travel about 200 miles round-trip and you won't make good time along those 200 miles either. Another example: it's 100 miles from Alpine to the park headquarters, even though it doesn't look far on a map.

A small repair shop is now doing business just west of Study Butte. But they won't be of much help when you have a vehicle problem 100 miles away, especially since cell phone coverage throughout the Big Bend is sporadic at best. Make sure your spare tire is in good shape, and you have jumper cables, and remember to carry water for your car as well as for yourself and your companions.

If you're going to travel off the paved road for any distance, you might want to toss a small shovel in the trunk, the military kind with the folding handle, in case you get stuck in sand or mud. It would also be a good idea to carry a spare alternator and fan belts and radiator hoses. Better safe than stranded. If you need a tow down here, you'll also need to take out a small loan.

Three routes lead into the Big Bend. Since Interstate Highway 10 is the main east/west thoroughfare close to Big Bend, the routes below begin there. However, U.S. Highway 90 dips lower into the Big Bend and offers better scenery, so check a map. All three of these routes intersect with U.S. 90 about an hour south of I-10.

✔ Route 1

Turn south onto U.S. 385 at Fort Stockton. This will take you to Marathon and into Big Bend National Park via the Persimmon Gap entrance. This is the least scenic of the routes, but the shortest if you're arriving from the east.

✔ Route 2

Turn south onto U.S. 67 about 10 miles west of Fort Stockton, following the highway into Alpine, then travel south on Texas Highway 118 into Study Butte (pronounced STOO-dy Byoot, by the way). This becomes an interesting road south of Alpine as the distant mesas gradually give way to the Chihuahuan Desert and, eventually, mountains.

✔ Route 3

Turn south onto Texas 17 at Balmorhea, through Fort Davis to Marfa, and then on to U.S. 67 south into Presidio, turning east on Farm Road 170 to Lajitas and on into Study Butte. This is probably the most scenic alternative, although it is also the most desolate once you are south of U.S. 90. Following this route also provides the opportunity to travel Farm Road 170, the River Road, one of the most scenic highways in Texas. A shorter variation of this route if you're arriving from the far west would be to turn south onto U.S. 90 at Van Horn to Marfa.

Repairs

If you have car trouble along the southern region of the Big Bend , the choices are limited. Terlingua Auto Repair near Study Butte, at (432) 371-2223, can handle most repairs and will provide tows, but understand that they might have to order a needed part from as far away as El Paso or Odessa. So what might take a couple hours in the city could take days out here.

Crime

As visitation has increased in the Big Bend over the past decade, so has crime. Incidents do occur. But to be realistic, your risk in an entire year is far, far less than one day in a city like Houston or Dallas, or even San

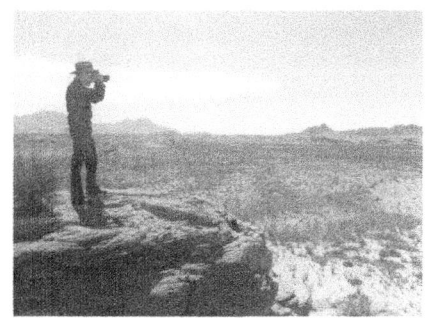

Angelo. It just seems worse out here because the area is otherwise so quiet and peaceful.

But remember, the Big Bend has been known since recorded history as being heavy with smugglers of one kind or another, whether it be drugs, whiskey, guns, cars, or candelilla—and the number of law enforcement officers in an area the size of some New England states is infinitesimal.

The best way to avoid conflict is to act and dress like a tourist, don't travel alone, and limit your explorations to well-traveled trails until you become much more familiar with the Big Bend.

9. LODGING

✔ **RVs**

Recreational vehicles are a convenient way to travel since you're driving or pulling your own lodging and kitchen, but to see Big Bend adequately you'll also need another vehicle since many of the mountainous roads simply will not accommodate RVs.

Several good RV parks are situated near the national park, mostly in the Study Butte area. In the park you'll be limited to the campground at Río Grande Village. The Lajitas Resort also has an RV park.

✔ **Tents**

If camping, a tent is necessary. The number of brands and types of tents available today is almost mind-boggling. Backpacking tents are now incredibly lightweight. But if you're car camping, you can pack as spacious a tent as you want.

Tents come in three main types:

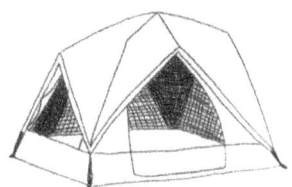

✔ **A-frame** — The most spacious of all tents and usually the least expensive and most difficult to set up. They come in a wide range of fabrics. Find something light and water resistant, with a sewn-in floor.

✔ **Dome** —This is either a regular dome or geodesic dome and is usually freestanding. They are relatively easy to set up and quite light, but can be almost as roomy as an A-frame. Almost all these are made of synthetic materials that don't breathe well at all. This can be a big problem in the desert at night when your body moisture collecting in the tent ceiling can actually create a small cloud that will drip your own sweat back down on you. Make certain the tent you get has plenty of ventilation, preferably on all four sides. Don't forget a rain-fly and that sewn-in floor.

✔ **Hammock Tents** — These ingenious devices were developed for the military and are a great idea. They keep you up off the ground, are ventilated all around, and provide rain shelter. However, they are meant for just one person, are very small, and you won't find many trees to tie one up on if you're in the desert.

✔ **Pop Tents** — A fairly recent invention, this clever tent looks like a large, flat disc when folded. Twist the sides and toss it into the air and suddenly it becomes a tent. Quite convenient, especially for car campers since they take up almost no space, just make sure it has a floor or bring a ground tarp with you.

✔ **Tunnel** — Small, with good wind- resistance but often difficult to set up. These are usually meant more for expeditions where space and weight are at a premium. Anyone car camping doesn't have to worry about those things.

✔ **Motels**

You may not want to rough it. Even if you do camp out most of your trip, it's nice to spend your last evening in a real room with all the conveniences of hot and cold running water and a soft bed so you'll be fresh and rested the next day for your long drive home.

You'll find motels in the Basin, at Study Butte, Terlingua, Lajitas, and Presidio, along with unusual accommodations in Big Bend Ranch State Park and near Ruidosa.

✔ **Big Bend Ranch State Park** — Nicknamed the Big House, the Sauceda ranch house on Big Bend Ranch State Park was built in 1908 and remodeled in the 1940s. It has three bedrooms and can accommodate eight persons. Kitchen privileges are available, or arrangements may be made for meals in the Sauceda Lodge dining area. For something a lot less fancy, check the Sauceda Lodge, a former hunting lodge built in the 1960s that sleeps 30 people in a segregated dormitory (married couples *are* separated). If you plan on spending much time at all in this park, you should either stay here or camp out since traveling the long, dirt road in and out each day will consume much of your precious vacation time even if you're staying in Presidio. The lodging is located in the heart of the park, many miles from a paved road, let alone a city, so you should definitely either bring your own meals or make arrangements to be fed while you're staying there. Call the park at (432) 229-3416.

✔ **Big Bend National Park** — The Chisos Mountain Lodge in the Basin has some secluded cottages, built by the Civilian Conservation Corps in the 1930s, and the views from some of them make any premium in cost worth it. Other units include the original motel strip built in the 1950s between the cabins and the restaurant, and a series of new multi-level buildings built toward the Window in the 1980s. Call long, long in advance for reservations. The Basin is a prized location and the units fill up quickly. This is especially true during spring break, Thanksgiving, and between Christmas and New Year's Day when you need to reserve rooms about a year ahead of time. Chili cook-off time the first weekend in November can also crowd area lodging. Call the lodge at (432) 477-2291.

✔ **Lajitas** — The resort at Lajitas is one of the nicest places to stay and eat in Big Bend outside of the national park. Originally built in the 1970s,

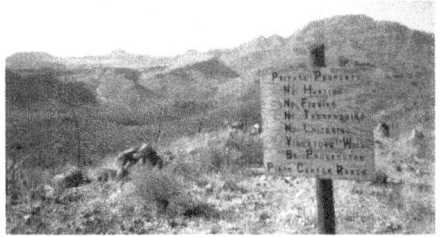

it replicates an Old West town and restored the historic Cavalry Post. The resort has more rooms than any other facility in the Big Bend and it has an RV park. You'll find several nice shops along its Boardwalk, a restaurant, a bakery, an 18-hole golf course, horse stables, and a large airstrip. As you might expect for a facility this classy, the rates are higher than any other in the area. And you are surrounded by beautiful scenery. The resort is situated right on the Rio Grande so don't miss walking down to the river at the historic Lajitas Crossing and noticing how narrow the river—an international border, remember—is here. The unofficial crossing here into Mexico, however, remains closed. Near the resort is the Barton Warnock Environmental Center, part of Big Bend Ranch State Park, a top place to visit to learn all about the history and geology of the area. Call them at (432) 424-5000.

✔ **Study Butte/Terlingua** —The motels in Study Butte and Terlingua have multiplied in number in recent years and they all offer comfortable and affordable places to rest your weary head outside of the parks. Once home only to Poncho's restaurant, a gas station and the Study Butte store, it has now become almost it's own small town. Poncho's and the Study Butte Store are gone, but Big Bend Resort provides motel rooms on both sides of the highway, an RV park, and a good café and convenience store in their gas station. The Big Bend Casitas, adjacent to Far Flung Tours, offer very nice cabins. Down the road, the Cottonwood Store stocks almost everything you will need, including many health-food items. You will find other restaurants, shops, a hardware store, a church, a liquor store, a car repair shop, and a horse remuda for those who would like to explore the area on a rent-a-pony. Get access here to the unusual, very accessible Indian Head area of the national park located at the junction of Farm Road 170 and Texas Highway 118. Study Butte or Terlingua are very convenient midway locations if you're planning on darting east into the national park and west into the state park or Presidio. You'll find a wide variety of lodging now in the Terlingua Ghost Town. Call Big Bend Casitas at (800) 839-7238. Call Big Bend Stables at (432)-371-3064. Call the Big Bend Resort and RV Park at (877) 386-4383. Call the Chisos Mining Company Motel (432) 371-2254. Call the El Dorado Motel (432) 371-2111. Call La Posada Milagro (432-371-3044). Call the Holiday Hotel (432) 201-1177.

✔ **Terlingua Ranch** — The Terlingua Ranch Lodge is an out-of-the-way place with a true taste of desert living—you've got to drive over 16 miles just to get there and once you're there, well, with apologies to Gertrude Stein, "There's not much there there." They've got a pool and restaurant, a gift shop, RV hookups and campsites. Although they may share the most famous name in Big Bend, don't confuse Terligua Ranch with Terlingua Ghost Town, or Terlingua Abaja for that matter. They are three very diffe-fent places, far away from each other (see Appendix C).

✔ **Campgrounds**

Campgrounds everywhere are on a first-come, first-served basis.

✔ **Big Bend Ranch State Park** — Camping Areas are located at Colorado Canyon, Madera Canyon, and at Grassy Banks River Access along Farm Road 170. Two group camping areas, Contrabando and Arenosa, are also along FM 170. The sites along the Río Grande all have self-composting toilets. Some small, primitive campgrounds may be found along the gravel park road in the heart of the park. No other facilities, electrical hookups, water, or dump stations are available in the park, and you should understand that most RVs will not be able to negotiate the jeep trails to backcountry park areas. Shower and restroom facilities are available at the Visitor's Center at La Sauceda Headquarters. Call the park at (432) 229-3416.

✔ **Big Bend National Park** —The Basin, again, is the most popular place, especially during the summer when it's about 20 degrees cooler than on the desert floor. It's also near many of the marked trails and the general store isn't far away. Cottonwood Campground is near the historic area of Castolon where there is also a store. Río Grande Campground is at Río Grande Village at the far eastern end of the park, also along the river. You'll find a store and gas station there, along with the park's only laundromat and only public showers. Primitive camping is available in other areas of the park. Primitive means everything from backpacking to just having no store near-by. The best of these is the Grapevine Hills, which you drive to directly on a dirt road — if the road's passable that day. You're away from the main road and the bustle of the three main campgrounds, and close to one of the best short hikes (see Top Hike 5) in the park. Call the park at (432)477-2251.

✔ **Outside the Parks** — You'll find RV parks on Terlingua Ranch, behind the Big Bend Motor Inn and the Study Butte RV Park—both at Study Butte—at BJ's between Study Butte and Terlingua, and at the Lajitas Resort in Lajitas. Find tent camping in style at Rancho Topanga near Lajitas, and at the very remote Chinati Hot Springs north of Ruidosa.

BIG BEND WEATHER

Month	Average Maximum (in F°)	Average Minimum (in F°)	Average Rain (in inches)
January	60.9	35.0	0.46
February	66.2	37.8	0.34
March	77.4	45.3	0.31
April	80.7	52.3	0.70
May	88.0	59.3	1.50
June	94.2	65.5	1.93
July	92.9	68.3	2.09
August	91.1	66.4	2.35
September	86.4	61.9	2.12
October	78.8	52.7	2.27
November	68.5	42.3	0.70
December	62.2	36.4	0.57

• Average yearly rainfall is 15.34 inches.
• Temperatures are 5-10 degrees lower in mountains, 5-10 degrees high along Rio Grande.

Source: National Parks Service

8. WEATHER

Sunshine is the one constant in Big Bend, but the weather can be surprisingly variable from one season to another and from one area to another. Some examples: One day in August I visited Río Grande Village on the river and noticed the temperature at the store was 120 degrees. A half-hour later in the Basin of the Chisos, I noticed the temperature was 78 degrees. That's about a 40-degree difference in a distance of about 30 miles. Another trip, in February, desert shrubs were blanketed with a heavy layer of frost early in the morning, but by noon the temperature was in the 80s.

Summer means temperatures in the low 100s on the desert during the day and remaining hot through the night. Day temperatures hover around 90 in the mountains. Winter (December through mid-February) means temperatures in the 30s to 60s, but sporadic heat waves into the 80s can happen on any winter day then drop dozens of degrees in a few minutes when a cold front — what Texans call "blue northers" — blasts through.

Contrary to what you might expect, May and June are the hottest months in Big Bend and most of the rain falls during the summer. Between June and October, sudden thunderstorms are common and flash floods will block traffic at low water crossings along roads outside the park. Don't worry when they do, just stop and enjoy the respite. The waters usually recede within a half-hour. Storm flooding once blocked roads in the park, too, but a few years ago the Park Service raised the elevation of the main road through the park so tourists wouldn't be inconvenienced.

7. WILDLIFE

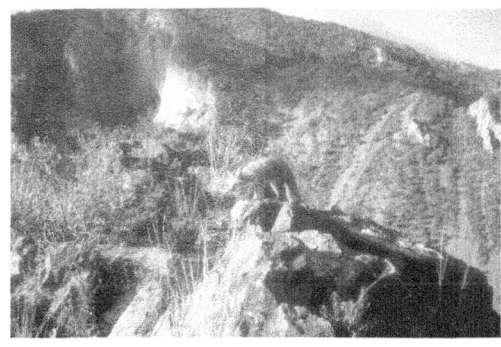

Wildlife abounds in Big Bend, especially in the park areas where animals have been protected for so many generations they don't have the fear of mankind animals in the wild usually have. You will often see javelinas and deer roaming around the Basin area in the national park, including in the parking lot of the motels, and on the mountain trails you might cross paths with a fox, bear or panther. In the desert, you'll see lizards and snakes, rabbits and roadrunners, scorpions and tarantulas, maybe an occasional coyote or pronghorn or bighorn sheep.

Birds abound — 450 species — and are a primary reason many people visit the park. It's exhilarating to see an eagle soaring below you as you rest on the South Rim of the Chisos, or a rare peregrine falcon swooping down for lunch, or glimpse a huge Mexican jay. Most birds can be found near the river, at springs like Dugout Wells or Boot Spring, or in the Chisos Mountains. Mexican jays and the rare Colima Warbler can be found in the U.S. only right here. Don't be surprised if you're eating at the Basin Lodge restaurant in the Spring and suddenly several tables empty as diners rush to the windows: these are birdwatchers and one of them has spotted that Lucifer's Hummingbird.

If you exercise common sense, and give the animals a little respect and distance, you shouldn't have any problems and the experience may be a memorable one. The most dangerous encounters can be those with bears, panthers, and venomous snakes or insects.

✔ Bears

Many black bears now call Big Bend National Park home, and over the past couple of years have been coming into increasing contact with human visitors. They're not out to get you, just your food. To do that, they have ripped open backpacks and tents and coolers.

To avoid problems just don't tempt the bears. Store all your food in the bear-proof lockers at designated campsites or lock it in the trunk of your car. Do the same with trash. Remember, ice chests aren't bear-proof, so do not leave them at your campsite or on the porch of your motel room. And if you are in a tent, do not leave a candy bar or some gorp lying around: a bear will sniff it out.

If you see a bear, keep your distance and don't feed it. This is especially true if you see cute, cuddly cubs. Mama is near and she doesn't like her kids playing with strangers. If the bear comes closer, try to scare it away by shouting or throwing rocks.

Report all sightings to a ranger.

✔ Mountain Lions

Panther attacks are rare, but a couple have happened since 1984. The Big Bend cats seem to like traveling the same trails hikers do, and they will stalk little children who appear to be alone so don't let them run ahead of you.

If you see a panther, you don't want to act like prey. That means no matter how frightened you may be, hold your ground and stand tall. Wave your arms and shout. Two or more people should get side-by-side; adults should lift children onto their shoulders, giving the impression to the cat that he is facing one large, dangerous animal. If the lion acts aggressively, throw stones.

Report all sightings to a ranger.

✔ Venomous Animals

Most of the snakes and insects you'll encounter here are harmless. Even those that can do you harm are just as interested in avoiding you as you are them. Far too many bites and stings occur when people try to capture or otherwise handle animals. Leave them alone.

Venomous snakes or insects will usually bite below the elbow or knee. That's because the victim has stepped or reached into a place he or she shouldn't have. The best way to avoid any such bites is to be very careful where you step or put your hands. Don't kick over a rotten tree with your foot to see what's under it. Watch where you're walking. I was wandering along an obscure trail in Green Gulch when a friend suddenly ordered me to freeze. I then heard that telltale rattle and when I looked down saw a coiled rattlesnake about a foot from my foot. I moved away slowly and cautiously, then continued on our hike. I realized that having a hiking stick with me would have been a good idea if the snake had decided to strike.

Don't reach into small caves. Look to make certain that the rock above your head you're about to grab doesn't have a sunning snake on it. If you're camping, shake out your sleeping bag before getting in at night, and shake out your boots before putting them on in the morning. Once a scorpion found a home in a towel and I was stung when I tossed the towel over my shoulder without looking.

Be wary of the velvet ant. You may see these large, beautiful, furry ants crawling along in the desert and be tempted to pick one up and to check it out closer. It's actually a wasp, just one that doesn't choose to fly, and it'll sting just as nasty as any other wasp.

A few words about Africanized honeybees are also in order. They have been tagged as "killer bees" because they are more aggressive than regular honeybees, and have killed hundreds of people in South and Central America. They are now in Texas. Their sting isn't any worse than any other bee, it's just that they're more cantankerous. More of them will sting and keep stinging longer and follow you farther to do it. They also get riled up quicker. If you happen to be allergic, this can present a serious problem and you shouldn't go to Big Bend without proper medication in case you are stung. The best defense is not to disturb any hives you see in the wild. If you are attacked, run and get to an enclosed area like a house or car. An average human can run faster than a bee can fly, so you can outrun them. It just takes longer to outrun Africanized bees than domesticated ones.

6. STUFF

You will need or may want several other items not noted previously. Among them:

✔ Binoculars

In an area as vast as the Big Bend, you will want the most powerful binoculars you can afford to see across those vistas.

✔ Books and Games

This might initially seem like an odd suggestion to bring with you to Big Bend, but if you've ever spent a day or two stranded in a motel room or tent because of a downpour, you'd know the value of being able to entertain yourself. This is especially true if you have children or teen-agers with you. Although some of the area motels now have television thanks to satellite technology, not all of them do.

✔ Cameras

Few places demand to be recorded as much as the scenery in Big Bend, especially when you get a clear day. If you're already an accomplished photographer, you know what equipment you're going to take. If you're shooting snapshots, don't spend a fortune on a camera with more bells and whistles on it than you can count. That expensive Nikon or Hasselblad won't take much better pictures than any other camera because, as most photographers eventually discover, 80 percent of the skill in taking pictures takes place about 8 inches behind the viewfinder. A point-and-shoot camera will do a good job unless you're shooting fine art landscapes. And it won't weigh much, either, fitting in a pocket or hip pack. Digital camera technology has made picture-taking very easy with cameras no larger than a deck of cards.

✔ Chairs

This is an often-overlooked luxury. When you find a place you might like to relax at and maybe have lunch, just put out a couple of chairs and relax in comfort. You can use folding lawn chairs or one of the new camp chairs that have backs supported by the seat and take up almost no space in a car, very little in a canoe, and not too much in a pack.

✔ Compass/GPS

Well, if you're doing mostly just day trips, or occasional hikes along marked paths, a compass isn't necessary unless you have a compulsion to know the precise direction you're always traveling in.

If you must have one, you can get an effective one that is relatively inexpensive. Buy the protractor style with transparent base plate and at least one straightedge. Of course, a compass isn't worth much without a map, a topographic map. A compass and map won't do you much good, however, if you don't know how to use them. Don't use a backcountry trip in the Big Bend as a learning experience.

Newer GPS technology is on the verge of replacing compasses in many uses. The global positioning system uses satellites to locate a user's exact position within 25 meters anywhere on Earth. These electronic units can now be held in your hand, and costs are now reasonable. It's a long-needed accessory for explorers, but it's mostly an expensive toy for day-trippers. Unless you get lost, when it can pinpoint your location on a map and even tell you which way to head to get back to the parking lot. But if you're going to rely on a GPS toy, make certain you know how to use before you wander off into the Big Bend. In fact, make certain you know how to use a compass and a map before your life depends on them, too.

✔ **Coolers**

An ice chest, or cooler, keeps snacks and drinks cold for you, a blessing in the Big Bend heat. Get one that fits easily in your car, is large enough for your needs, and that is not made of Styrofoam. Styrofoam squeaks like crazy, especially over many of the types of roads you'll be driving on, and it breaks up easily.

✔ **Insect Repellent**

You really won't need insect repellent unless you're going to be hiking in the Chisos Mountains in the Spring. Then take a lot mosquito spray. I had a white shirt ruined by bloodstains after a hike to the South Rim thanks to the hordes of mosquitoes I fed along the way. Military recommendations are to use a repellent with a lot of DEET; 30 percent is supposed to be about right.

✔ **Guide Books**

Big Bend has the best guidebooks available for any national park. You already have this guide, so you're well prepared to plan your trip. You can also find other guides, ones with detailed descriptions of trails and every roadside stop in the park, like the Big Bend Natural History Association's two Road Guides and their Hikers Guide that are bargains. *(See Appendix A.)*

✔ **Hiking Staffs**

Many people swear by hiking staffs or poles and others never use them. I find I use mine in some situations, not in others. I don't much like to carry one when I am on more or less level ground or if I'm going to have to use my hands a lot to scramble up and down rocks. However, on hikes like the South Rim or Lost Mine Peak or Mule Ears Spring, a staff can provide the stability of a third leg. And some double as monopods for cameras.

Staffs come in all sorts of styles and materials. You can find them in a variety of woods, aluminum, even sotol. I think most wood is too heavy to tote around all day, so I use aluminum or sotol. I use the aluminum staff when I need the stability a monopod provides for my camera: the staff's top knob twists off to provide a base for the camera. You can find sotol staffs at most shops in Big Bend and they make for a great walking accessory because they are tough, flexible and extremely light.

✔ **Hip Packs/Day Packs**

Also called a fanny or lumbar pack, these are large pockets, or small purses, sewn into a wide belt and are one of the great inventions of mankind. You can carry a large assortment of things in one, depending on the size, including an emergency rain parka, first aid supplies, 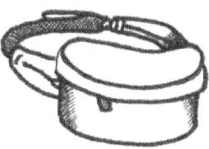 snacks, pocket knife, car keys, etc. The wide belt can carry a water bottle in a bottle parka, or two. Just make sure to buy one with a long enough belt so that you can pull it back and tie it off since most hip-pack buckles slip over time when the pack or belt is loaded down.

A good alternate for a hip pack, especially if you're to be carrying heavy water bottles and cameras, is to go to a police supply shop and buy a nylon equipment belt. They're relatively cheap and extremely sturdy. Buy a big pouch for the belt and you'll have as much storage space as a fanny pack and the ability to carry a lot more on the belt. I also discovered that a matching nylon handcuff case makes a perfect compass case.

Small daypacks have become more popular in recent years, especially those packs that also carry a water bladder. Camelback is a popular brand. I don't particularly care for them because I don't like weight pulling on my shoulders, but that's a personal prejudice. Wear what you're comfortable with.

✔ **Knives**

A small pocketknife is a handy thing to have. If you get one with multiple blades, it can serve any number of uses, including as part of a first aid kit since some have tweezers and scissors. Some even have forks and spoons. You don't need to pretend you're Jim Bowie, so leave the hog stickers at home.

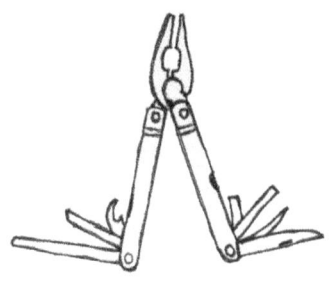

Multi-tool knives (Leatherman is the best known brand) offer such devices as pliers and a saw and a knife blade and screwdrivers, etc. that all fold together into a compact package. A number of companies make different versions in prices ranging from around $10 (at a discount store like Target or Wal-Mart) to around $60. I like 'em.

✔ **Neckerchief**

That little piece of cloth to wrap around your neck can be one of the best things to take along. It keeps your neck shaded and can be pressed into service as a cap in an emergency. If you keep it wet, the evaporating water will cool the back of your neck and keep your body much cooler. You can also find things called cool ties that are neckerchiefs with synthetic material sewn inside that acts like an ice pack, keeping you even cooler. You just immerse it in cold water or freeze it overnight, and its coolness will last a while into the heat of the day.

✔ **Phones**

Cell phones have only sporadic service in Big Bend, so you may find more use for yours as a camera rather than for communications.

✔ **Plastic Bags**

Unless you know you will always be eating at a developed picnic area or in a restaurant, bring along a few plastic bags to pack your trash and garbage in. Don't leave it behind.

✔ **Sunglasses**

I've heard arguments about the worth of sunglasses, and I think in casual use they're more a fashion statement than a necessity. But in the desert, a quality pair is useful to protect your eyes from glare and ultraviolet light. Glare is a problem both in the desert and on the river. Big Bend has a lot of ultraviolet light shining down, which can harm the eyes. Look for a pair that is sturdy, with lightweight plastic lenses that block the ultraviolet. They won't be cheap, but, hey, these are your eyes we're talking about. You might also want to opt for one of those funky eyeglass straps that will keep the glasses on your head, or around your neck when you don't have them on. This is especially important when you're on the river.

✔ **Sunscreen**

I hate to sound cruel, but anyone who goes off into the desert without proper sunscreen on them deserves the pain they'll feel that night. If you haven't gotten the idea yet, Big Bend is a hot place, with sun shining much more often than not, even in winter. Slather on the sunscreen, the higher the SPF rating the better. This really isn't the place to go for a tan.

Tanning might give you what people a few decades ago called a healthy glow, but will certainly eventually give your skin that attractive leathery look by the time you're middle-aged if you tan regularly. If you must tan, go to the beach or a pool where you can cool off in the water when it gets too hot. Cool water is a precious and rare commodity in Big Bend.

But if you simply must go home with a tan to prove to friends you've spent your vacation out of doors, don't worry. In summertime, you will get a tan almost regardless of the amount of sunscreen you use if you spend any time at all outside.

5. FIRST AID

If you're just a casual visitor to Big Bend, and you're not going off into the backcountry or across the desert for days at a time, you don't need a huge first aid kit but you should carry a few essentials.

Remember that this is still a primitive area. The nearest medical clinic is in Alpine, 100 miles away. The nearest medical center is in Midland/Odessa, 250 miles away. Terlingua Medics have a fine emergency medical technician staff, but they are limited in numbers and equipment and access — they are on call in an area larger than 2,000 square miles with few roads.

So even if you're just traveling around by car, you need a few first aid items handy. If you're taking one of the hikes, stuff the items in a fanny pack or accessory pocket on a belt or backpack. Here's a suggested ✔ check list:

- ❑ Adhesive tape.
- ❑ Antibacterial ointment.
- ❑ Antiseptic soap or wipes.
- ❑ Antacid.
- ❑ Aspirin or ibuprofen to alleviate pain and inflammation.
- ❑ Band-Aids, about four each of assorted sizes.
- ❑ Blister pads or moleskin.
- ❑ Butterfly Band-Aids.
- ❑ First aid booklet.
- ❑ Gauze pads.
- ❑ Matches, waterproof or a disposable lighter.
- ❑ Needle.
- ❑ Personal medications.
- ❑ Razor blade.
- ❑ Scissors.
- ❑ Sunscreen.
- ❑ Toothache relief medication, such as oil of cloves
- ❑ Tweezers.

4. CLOTHING

When the summer sun beats down on you in Big Bend, you're going to be tempted to make like a Mescalero and shed as many of your clothes as possible. Resist this urge. You'll see a number of locals, usually guides, who wear short shorts and either tank tops or light T-shirts, but they've lived here for a long time. You just got here. If you're coming from a city with a climate that is routinely hot, like Houston or Miami, you might think you can handle the Big Bend heat. You might do better than someone from Portland—Oregon or Maine—but this is still a special place with no air conditioning and a dry heat that can fake you into thinking it isn't nearly as hot as it really is. Face it: You aren't as acclimated to the desert climate as a river guide or an old onion farmer from Ojinaga. It may not be stylish, but long sleeves and full-length pants are the way to go in the summer. They will protect you from the sun, cactus and insects better than shorts and T-shirts. The sun here will bake a fair city-person's skin in a half-hour. Or less.

Take a good look at Mexicans in this neck of the desert: even when working outside in the summer they wear long trousers and long-sleeved shirts and wide brimmed hats. They do this for a good reason. They have many generations' worth of experience in this desert.

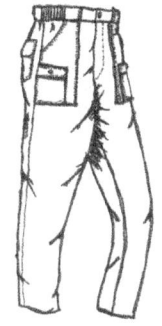

The weather here from April through October is fairly consistent: hot, hotter, then back to hot. During those months, you don't need to be always second-guessing the weather. You know it's hot and that you might get a short shower. Dress accordingly, which means if you don't want to get wet, carry a rain jacket or poncho in a fanny pack or small backpack when you're away from your car for any time.

The other months are wildly unpredictable, ranging from below freezing to the 80s in the space of a few hours. The way to dress then is to dress in layers so you can regulate your comfort. Let me give you an example. On an early March morning you dress in underwear, T-shirt, regular shirt, and hooded sweatshirt or jacket, hiking pants, hat. You cover your head with the hood, holding it down with your hat, and step out into the cold morning. As the hours wear on and the sun rises, you drop the hood, unzip the jacket, eventually removing the jacket altogether. If it gets even hotter during the afternoon, you might unbutton or remove the shirt. As the day cools, you reverse the process. Wearing a pair of those convertible trousers with legs that unzip just above the knee to become shorts, gives you an even greater range of options if you just have to wear shorts.

Fiber Choices

Generally speaking, clothing made of natural fibers is best.

✔ Cotton

Cotton breathes well and is light. In tropical areas around the world, you'll find people wearing cotton more than all other fabrics combined. Its only drawback is that it loses any insulating properties it might have the instant it is wet, and it dries quite slowly. So cotton makes for terrible socks in the desert, bad underwear, but OK shirts and trousers.

✔ **Hemp**

This fabric is making a small comeback, but not too many items are made from it as yet. It has some of the same qualities as both cotton and wool, being light but losing its insulation slowly. Some weaves can be as rough as wool, others light as linen.

✔ **Wool**

This is the warmest and will absorb up to 30 percent of its weight in water without losing its insulating properties. But wool is rough and heavy, very heavy when wet. Most woolens are not good for Big Bend except in the coldest of winter, however some new wool blends and lightweight alpaca wools make for almost perfect socks.

✔ **Silk**

Often overlooked, silk is an almost magical fiber. It's the second warmest natural fiber, yet is very light. But, like cotton, it loses its insulation quickly when wet. Worn under other garments, it traps heat remarkably well. Worn alone, it becomes cool. Silk also feels great against the skin.

✔ **Synthetics**

These fake fibers, most some proprietary formula of plastic, are quite popular these days but some aren't worth the extra cost. Most of them were designed for colder weather. In winter they can be a good choice in Big Bend since they insulate well and are far lighter than wool. Some synthetic fleeces feel wonderful.

Capilene, one synthetic, is a good alternate for silk or cotton underwear. It's a form of polyester fiber that absorbs water on one side but repels it on the other, wicking moisture away from your body and spreading it out over a large area that will evaporate more quickly and keep you drier.

Some companies are now making short- and long-sleeved shirts of other sorts of synthetics that boast of actually keeping your skin cool in severe heat. Long-sleeved and vented fishing shirts of this material are carried by many sporting goods stores.

3. SHOES

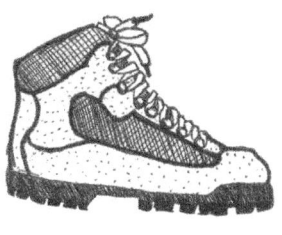

Apache legend says that when God made the world, He gathered up all the leftover debris and chucked it into the Big Bend. You'll believe it if you walk more than a few yards off any maintained trail. Some of the desert you see here might look flat, but it's not. From the desert to the mountains, Big Bend is hard and rough, even unstable in some places. To help you get around well and to avoid sore feet and a sore back at the end of a day, even if you just do easy walks, you need sturdy, ankle-supporting shoes.

✔ **Cowboy Boots**

If you're riding a horse, fine. Otherwise, forget it. Cowboy boots were designed to fit properly into stirrups, and to protect the lower leg. I've known some hikers who swore by them, but they always complained of sore feet that evening even if they never admitted to those sore feet after the trip was over. You just can't scramble around Big Bend all day in cowboy boots.

✔ **Dress or Casual Shoes**

Forget them. Leather soled shoes have no place out here, and even the gum-soled shoes won't be kind to your feet. And they have no ankle support and little arch support.

✔ **Hiking Shoes**

These are the only shoes to wear in Big Bend. Period. Trust me. Carve it in stone. Some hiking shoes are meant for rugged, mountainous use in more northern climes and are made completely of leather. They're good, of course, but for Big Bend you'll be better off with a hiking boot that is framed in leather but with as many fabric inserts as possible to let your feet breathe. You don't have to pay an arm and a leg for a good pair. Just make sure you get something with decent ankle support, lug soles, solid laces, and that fit perfectly. When you go to the store to try on a pair, bring the socks you will be wearing on your hikes, not your everyday socks.

✔ **High-heels**

This is a joke. Right?

✔ **Sandals**

These open-toed shoes might feel much cooler than shoes or boots, and they might be OK when you're on the river, but don't use them for hiking here. Sandals come in an almost endless variety, from simple beach thongs to Mexican leather huaraches to plastic Crocs and their copies to fancy leather to the more recent hiking sandals that provide almost as much support and coverage as a hiking boot but still leave some skin exposed.

On one trip, my wife ended up with a 3-inch cactus thorn stuck in her foot. That thorn went through the leather portion of a hiking boot and two layers of socks. Imagine how deep it might have gone if it had started its journey on her skin instead of the boot's.

✔ **Running Shoes**

This is another of those broad categories, including everything from simple canvas shoes to those pricey, pumped-up, neon-colored, strapped and zippered, spring-loaded, leather and synthetic, multi-purpose shoes that the cooler folk don't even bother to tie up. Running and cross-training shoes aren't bad here, at least if you won't be going off the beaten path much. But they weren't made for the sort of abuse they'll get in Big Bend. Shoes in this category are made with the assumption that your feet will be on level ground, whether it be a running track, a basketball court, a tennis court, or a boat deck. Nothing is level in Big Bend. Your feet will be forced in various directions at the same time, and you'll get a lot of stress around your ankles. In the meantime, the desert rock will begin ripping up your soles.

Blisters

A couple of tips:

• Make sure to carry a blister kit with you at all times. This should preferably be a couple patches of moleskin, antiseptic cream and a sterile razor or pin to pierce the blister. Adhesive bandages will suffice if you don't have any moleskin. As soon as you feel a hot spot, stop and treat it.

• Wear two pairs of socks, or a pair of hiking socks made with two layers.

Wear an inner pair of silk or, preferably, lightweight polypropylene socks and an outer pair of wool, a wool blend, or heavier polypro. Blisters are created from friction and the two layers of socks will be doing most of the rubbing back and forth instead of your feet against your boots

2. HATS

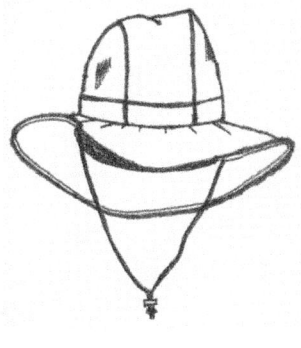

Dehydration and heat exhaustion and heat stroke are the primary dangers when traveling in Big Bend and they're the reasons why you should always wear a hat, the proper sort of hat, when walking about in the desert.

Before 1960, people rarely went out of doors without some sort of hat on their heads. Then it all changed. Some experts say to blame John Kennedy, who was inaugurated in fiercely cold with his head bare. After all, why hide all that abundant hair, especially when the outgoing president was so bald?

They say Kennedy's dislike of hats ended the trend. Others blame the nearly universal use of air conditioning, although I'm unclear how cooling homes and offices would mean folks wouldn't want to wear hats outside. Regardless, many people today just don't like hats. If you're one of them, get over it, especially in Big Bend. Cowboys don't wear their Stetsons and vaqueros don't wear their sombreros just to look good singing on stage.

Heat will literally boil your brain in its own juices. In the desert, you simply have to keep your head in cooling shade in order to survive. Also, you lose much of your body heat through your head, most of it during winter when your chest is usually well-covered. Wearing a hat in the cold will actually keep your feet warm.

A hat is the second most important thing you can have in the desert, after water. Buy a good one that fits perfectly.

Among your hat options are:

✔ Baseball Caps

Also called "gimme caps" in Texas because they are often emblazoned with a company logo and were given out to clients who said, "Hey, gimme one them caps." Gimme caps and caps with the logos of popular sports teams — especially the Dallas Cowboys hereabouts — are very popular, but not too practical in the desert. Their long bills are good for keeping sun off your face, but they leave the neck and ears exposed. Adding a handkerchief at the back helps. That's what the French Foreign Legion did in the Sahara. A couple companies even make caps just this way, with detachable drapes. This is better than a plain baseball cap, but, let's face it, those flaps make you look like a dweeb and if you don't like hats to begin with you're going to like these even less. Also, any sort of ball cap still leaves your ears exposed and that thin skin and cartilage will burn up real good.

✔ Cowboy Hats

The best hats are those that were developed for this kind of climate: broad-brimmed cowboy hats and sombreros. Their wide brims keep your face, ears and neck in shade; the tall crowns with vents allow air to circulate around your head. Remember that darker shades retain heat more than lighter shades, so pretend you're a good guy and wear a white hat in the summer and be a bad guy with a black hat in winter. Add a "stampede string" to help keep your chapeau on your cranium when the weather gets windy.

Another thing to note is that wide-weave straw hats are not much better than no hat at all. They don't shade enough, although they might feel cooler. Tightly woven straw hats, like some Mexican sombreros or Panama hats, are the best if you prefer straw. And stay away from cheap wool versions like those sold at many discount stores. A lightweight, quality felt is best.

✔ Fedoras

I'm including just about all short-brimmed hats in this category. Dozens of types are out there, good and bad. Some floppy, some stiff. Some felt, some wool, some canvas or cotton or synthetic fabric. Some brands are specially made for outdoor travel and hiking and come in light colors and in lightweight fabrics. Some are designed to float, making them a great river hat. They're certainly better than caps, but I still prefer the broader brim on a cowboy hat for the desert.

✔ **Visors**

Mostly worthless out here. Although they shade your eyes and part of your face, they leave your head exposed. Some versions come with scarves attached to go over your head, and those are better but not by much because they don't have room for air to circulate around your head.

1. FOOD and WATER

You're going into a desert. You need water

This seems obvious, but too many times I've witnessed people striding across the desert carrying no water or an insufficient supply. People have died out here from lack of water. Take this admonition seriously.

The Chihuahuan Desert is one of four warm deserts in North America, along with the Great Basin, the Mojave and the Sonoran. The Chihuahuan sprawls in Texas between El Paso and Pecos and deep into Mexico. This is a relatively high desert with the lowest areas being about 1,000 feet above sea level while the highest exceed 7,500 feet. Mountains on three sides block the rain, and the fourth side is nothing but semi-arid plains.

Rainfall varies from 7.5 inches to 12 inches in a year. Temperatures are high. At mid-day in the summer, ground temperatures can reach 180 degrees.

Rain usually begins in June and lasts into the fall. Summer is hot with warm nights, and sudden storms are common. The storms are generally over quickly, providing good entertainment, but can also cause flash floods. Fragrances released after a desert rainstorm are an unparalleled experience. Winter days can be warm, but the nights get very cold. Winter storms can also be unexpected, bringing sudden drops in temperatures and freezing rain or snow.

As you can probably figure out, you're going to need a lot of water while you're here. This is especially true if you spend any time at all hiking or walking about.

✔ **Springs and Tinajas**

A tinaja is an indentation in stone, sometimes very deep but often shallow, in which rainwater collects, providing uncertain water supplies for desert dwellers. But springs and tinajas are unreliable and usually unsafe to drink so you shouldn't depend on them even if they are marked on a map. If you're hiking in the backcountry, ask a ranger about available water before you head out.

If you insist on drinking water from these desert sources, or from the river or creeks, make sure to treat it before imbibing. Remember that the Río Grande from El Paso to the Gulf of Mexico is mostly used to dump raw sewage or toxic waste into. A number of microorganisms that may make their home in these waters can cause severe illnesses like giardiasis, shigellosis, amebiasis, typhoid or cholera. Bringing water to a rolling boil for more than a minute will kill most parasites and bacteria. Water can also be treated with iodine. Filters also work, but take care to get a high quality one with a small enough filter (0.2 microns or smaller) to block most of those nasty microorganisms.

✔ **Dehydration**

Most people don't drink enough water. Don't wait until you're thirsty to drink some; by then you're already suffering from some degree of dehydration. You will need to drink a *minimum* of 1 gallon of water per person per day in the summer. You can get by on a little less in winter—more if you're exercising heavily. The general rule of thumb is to drink a half-quart before you start out for the day, then drink at least a half-pint of water every 30 minutes.

Remember that dehydration leads to heat exhaustion. Heat exhaustion leads to heat stroke. Heat stroke leads to permanent damage to your brain, kidneys and liver. And it'll kill you. A few years ago, a deputy U.S. marshal died of exposure here and he wasn't even hiking across the desert. His car broke down on a dirt road. He didn't have enough water to survive another day.

Dehydration causes headaches, discomfort, a drop in physical performance and increases your risk of heart problems. Dark urine means you're dehydrated. You can lose more than a quart of body fluid through sweating in an hour of exercise.

Heat exhaustion symptoms include weakness, headaches, nausea, faintness, breathlessness, loss of appetite, rapid pulse and cool skin. Rest in the shade if you find any, drink water or a watered down sport drink (one-quarter strength).

Heat stroke makes you confused and disoriented, you lose coordination and your skin becomes hot. Cool down quickly, move to shade, pour on water, fan air across yourself, remove clothing, massage arms and legs, place ice packs at neck, armpits and groin, immerse in cool water—anything to rapidly lower body temperature. Get medical attention as soon as possible.

In addition to drinking lots of water and/or electrolyte-laced sports drinks like Gatorade and Powerade, you can help prevent dehydration by getting plenty of rest. A lack of sleep or strenuous exercise increases your risk of heat exhaustion and stroke.

On a hot summer day, a nice cool beer can be awfully tempting. As Alfonso Bedoya says to Gregory Peck in the classic Western *The Big Country*: "Don't do it!" Alcohol is one of the worst things you can drink in the heat. It interferes with the body's ability to cool itself and impairs judgment. You want neither in the desert. Save the brews until evening in your cabin, hotel room, or at a restaurant.

Be aware that some medications can be just as bad as alcohol.

Best thing to do is buy a five-gallon water cooler to keep in your car, keep it well stocked with ice and fill it every morning before you head out. Fill canteens or bottles or small containers with ice in the morning as well, keeping them topped off with water from the cooler whenever you stop the car.

Don't walk anywhere without some water.

Carrying Water

You have several options on how to carry water.

✔ Botas

Once the choice of hippies—you remember hippies, they're in all the history books—you can look quite cool zapping a precise stream of water into your mouth from a bota. Originally made from goat innards, these are now made from vinyl and sometimes are covered with sueded leather. They don't

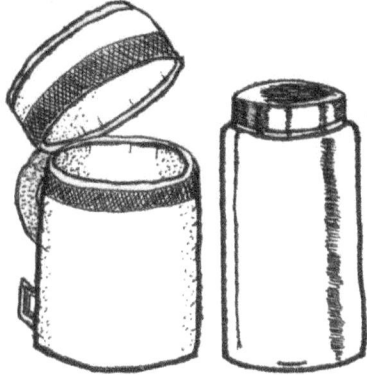

carry much, their straps tend to be thin so as to cut into your shoulder, and their small mouths make it difficult to get ice in.

✔ Bottle Carriers

A relatively new device, this pocket on the end of a strap or carabiner allows you to stick in a bottle of designer water so you can carry your Evian or Perrier or Clearly Canadian with you. They may look good, but they're impractical for desert walks of any length simply because they can't be kept cool. Nothing like a gulp of hot peach-flavored water to make you want to gag.

✔ Canteens

The old-fashioned cowboy canteens work well, especially if you can spare the water or are near enough to streams to keep soaking their blanketed sides. Water evaporating from the blanket keeps the water inside cooler. A strap allows you to carry a canteen across your shoulder. The military canteen also works fine, except they tend to be smaller than the 2-quart cowboy canteens. These usually attach to a belt. Both types are difficult to fill with ice.

✔ Hydration Packs

A relatively new invention, these water-filled backpacks have become hugely popular with hikers. Their tubes loop around to a hiker's mouth and a quick sip may be had by using the bite valve at the end of the tube. Except for the cooler months, I don't like them at all. You can carry more water on your back than you can comfortably carry around your waist or over your shoulder, but too many of these packs don't have wide enough mouths for ice nor are they insulated very well. And you're desperately going to need ice in any water you carry. I also don't care for all that sloshing going on behind me. If you like them, make certain to inspect it completely and find one with a wide mouth.

✔ **Water Bottles**

My water carrier of choice. You can buy these clear plastic bottles at any outdoor store, then get an insulated jacket to zip them in and carry on your belt. The pioneers in this field, and still the best, are Outdoor Research's Water Bottle Parkas in either 1 or 2-quart sizes, but more companies are getting into the market now. Go for the 2-quart bottle. They are convenient, have wide mouths to allow easy packing of ice, and will keep your water cooler than any other device short of carrying an Igloo cooler on your back.

✔ **Water Jugs**

I've actually seen people hiking to the Chimneys, across the desert, carrying a store-bought 2-gallon jug of water. It was enough water for the hike, but I imagine that jug could get very heavy in the hiker's hand before he walked too far, and the water could get quite warm. Other jug options include collapsible plastic versions of varying quantities, but they all have the same problem: they have to be carried by hand.

Car Water

And don't just carry enough drinking water, remember your car. Vehicles overheat with great regularity out here and having enough water in your vehicle for the radiator could save you a very long walk and might even save your life.

Food

If you're cooking your own food, you have a number of options. I won't go into the backpacker stoves here, they're more specialized than you need if you're at an accessible campsite or picnicking for lunches.

Fires can be a serious problem in an area as dry as Big Bend usually is, and wood fires are prohibited in the national park; the state park requires a fire pan. Use charcoal in the stands at campgrounds or a Coleman-type double burner.

Most likely, you'll have a picnic lunch somewhere by the side of the road or along a trail. That means either sandwiches or some sort of dry mix.

If you're buying your own food, I'd recommend stopping at one of the supermarkets in Alpine or Presidio to stock up. The selection is as varied as in any large city and prices are lower than you'll pay in the park area. Once you're in Big Bend, your choices are limited and the prices high.

Outside the parks, you can find groceries at the gas station or Cottonwood Store in Study Butte, the Terlingua Store near the Ghost Town, and the convenience store in Lajitas.

Inside the national park, you can find groceries at stores in Río Grande Village, Castolon and the Basin, but they don't stock much. The Basin general store, though, is the only place south of Midland where you can find a decent selection of camping supplies.

If you're like most visitors, you'll be looking for restaurants.

✔ The Chisos Mountain Lodge Restaurant

The Chisos Mountain Lodge in the Basin has been in operation almost as long as the park has. It offers a great view and nourishing food. They will also make you a box lunch to take on a trail during the day. Call (432) 477-2291.

✔ La Kiva

La Kiva is a funky little place you descend into just past the Terlingua Creek bridge. A new owner has had to remodel the place and the food here has varied wildly over the years. Sometimes they offered none, sometimes just barbecue, sometimes luscious steaks and exotic fare. You just never know, and that's part of its charm. Even if you don't eat at La Kiva, you have to stop by at least for a drink and to drink in the underground atmosphere. Call (432) 371-2250.

✔ The Patio

The Patio restaurant in Presidio is almost worth the long drive just to eat lunch or dinner there. It's an unassuming little place with Mexican food so good it's been pleasing locals for decades. If you make a day trip along the River Road, to Fort Leaton, or out to the remote reaches of Big Bend Ranch State Park, this is the perfect place to end your day. Call (432) 229-4409.

✔ Starlight Theatre

The Starlight Theatre restaurant in Terlingua Ghost Town has established a significant reputation and the food has always been the best. The restaurant is a restored movie theater dating back to the quicksilver mining days, hence its name. Check out the vast cowboy campfire mural on the back wall. You'll also find performers entertaining the crowd here some nights. Call (432) 371-2326.

✔ Others

You'll find several other restaurants in the general Terlingua area, but many come and go with alarming regularity. However, the café at the gas station of the Big Bend Resort in Study Butte has always served up good food, and the funky outdoor **Espresso y Poco Mas** café in Terlingua Ghost Town has a great reputation, especially for breakfasts.

You can also find a liquor store in Study Butte.

Long Draw Pizza (432) 371-2608, along Farm Road 170 just past the Ghost Town, is a place that's been around for quite a while. It's usually open only on weekends, however, and if you're hungry, either go early or call ahead because they make everything from scratch and it gets very popular with locals on Friday or Saturday evenings, so you could wait very long for your pizza.

The **Candelilla** restaurant (432) 424-5000 in Lajitas is undergoing changes with its new ownership. Still maintaining a gourmet flavor, it's becoming more affordable with such typical fare as chicken-fried steaks and fajitas.

The **Bad Rabbit Café** at Terlingua Ranch Lodge (432) 371-2416) is fairly basic and quality depends greatly on who happens to be cooking. It also suffers from being located on Terlingua Ranch so far from a main road, but if you're staying at the lodge, add it to your agenda. There's occasionally live music, so inquire.

The **Reata** in Alpine (432) 837-9232, open only in evenings, serves gourmet cowboy cuisine, from jalapeño soup to fried alligator and pepper-crusted tenderloin with port wine sauce. Also in Alpine is **La Trattoria** for Italian fare (432) 837-2200.

In Marathon, the **Café Cenizo** located in the Gage Hotel is one of the best eateries in the entire area, set in a beautiful courtyard of the historic hotel with indoor and outdoor fireplaces (432) 386-4510. Breakfasts can be exceptional.

PART TWO
TOP 10 HIKES

Never pass up a chance to sit down or relieve yourself.
— Apache saying

Big Bend National Park has always offered a wide assortment of hikes, from short to long, easy to strenuous, accessible to relatively inaccessible. It even has some secret hikes not marked on maps or with road signs or in park guides. I'm not telling anyone about my secret places. Go find your own. You'll hear about them from rangers, locals, or fellow travelers you might meet on your trip. Strike up a conversation.

Until just recently, Big Bend Ranch State Park's 300,000 acres were accessible to visitors only on guided trips. That's now changed and the park has opened several trails and roads to the public, increasing the number of excellent and interesting hikes you'll find in the Big Bend.

The Big Bend area has hundreds of miles of hiking trails crossing the national parks, the state parks, and private property. I'm not including the private trails here because you should respect private property even if it appears vast and empty. If you want to hike on some of them, do a little work and ask permission first.

Also, because this book is meant to be used by a first-time visitor, I'm not including several of the more primitive or difficult routes, even though a couple of them may be better than the ones listed below. Even if you're an experienced hiker or backpacker, you should get some experience in the unique ecosystems of the Big Bend before you tackle some of the more remote and strenuous trails.

The hikes listed below will take you through the desert, into the mountains, and by the river, and range from the relatively easy to the more difficult. Also, they are all day hikes so you can still run away to the comfort of a soft bed and a warm shower when the sun goes down.

10. OJITO ADENTO, BIG BEND RANCH STATE PARK

Any time you can relax by a waterfall in the middle of the desert, you should. This is an easy 1.5-mile round-trip walk through desert scrub to a grove of cottonwood trees by Bofecillos Creek. Continuing east along the creek will take you over some boulders, then to the spring and a small waterfall.

The name literally means "small spring inside," probably referring to the fact that accessing the falls takes you inside a canyon.

The trailhead is well marked, to the north of the main interior park road, about 8.5 miles west of La Sauceda.

9. CINCO TINAJAS, BIG BEND RANCH STATE PARK

This is a relatively easy 2-mile roundtrip hike to a slot canyon where five waterholes (hence the name) line up before the land gives way to a broad plain of desert.

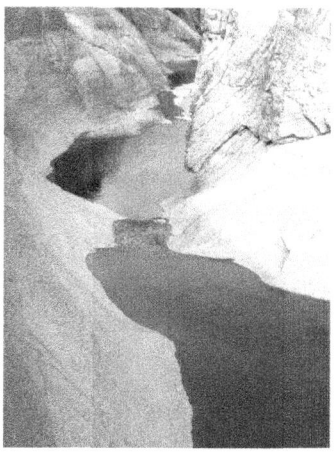

Almost all the rain that falls near here drains over a 15-foot drop into this narrow, short canyon made of dense volcanic rock. Over millions of years, a small tributary of Leyva Creek has eroded the rock into these five depressions. You can view the tinajas from either side of the creek, just pay attention to the map at either the trailhead or get one from the Visitor Center at La Sauceda or Fort Leaton or the Barton Warnock Center. You can also scramble around to one side and up the hill that creates the narrow canyon for an excellent view looking down at the tinajas and out over the desert.

The canyon rim overlooking the tinajas also provides incredible panoramas of the far reaches of the park. You can see the Bofecillos highlands, flat-topped La Mota mountain, the Cienega Mountains, Oso Peak, and Fresno Peak on the rim of the Solatario. If the skies are clear, you can even make out the Sierra Rica in Mexico and the Chisos Mountains in the national park far away.

Given all the options available at the tinajas, it's a great place for kids to climb and run off a lot of energy—just don't leave them alone.

This trailhead is also well marked, again to the north of the main park road, about 1.3 miles west of La Sauceda.

8. SANTA ELEÑA CANYON, BIG BEND NATIONAL PARK

I'd rate the 1.7-mile round trip trail into the mouth of Santa Eleña Canyon as moderately strenuous because on the return trip the trail is rather steep, but it's worth it. In actuality, this is more of a walk than a hike. If you can, arrive in early morning when the sun lights up the canyon walls for a great photo. The rest of the day, much of the canyon will be in shadow.

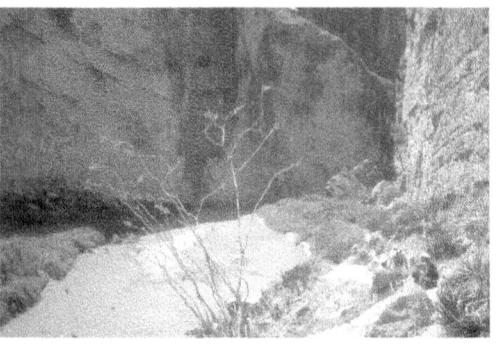

This is one of those hikes that nearly everyone is capable of doing and that everyone should do because it demonstrates in clear detail just how varied a desert can be regardless of whatever stereotype you have in mind. Also, it takes you into a seemingly mysterious canyon formed by the most famous river in Texas. It's a life-sustaining river that is an international boundary with no soldiers on either side, just those sheer canyon walls towering above you.

The interesting, well-marked trail begins at the mouth of Santa Eleña Canyon. To get to the trail leading into the canyon you must first cross Terlingua Creek. Yes, you'll get your feet wet. Unless there has been a very recent storm, Terlingua Creek is rarely more than shin deep, so tie your hiking boots around your neck and enjoy the cool wade. But be aware of the weather. Terlingua Creek can flood quickly and if it does after you've crossed it you will be trapped on the hillside in the canyon.

Once you cross Terlingua Creek, climb up the steps and switchbacks on the face of the Mesa de Anguila to a cliff overlooking the fertile Río Grande plain to the east and the deep canyon below you and to the west. You then follow the trail into the canyon itself, watching the terrain change from rock to river grasses. You can then lounge on one of the many huge rocks, getting sun or relaxing as you listen to the rushing river.

The trailhead begins just below the parking area marked for Santa Eleña Canyon at the end of Ross Maxwell Drive in the national park. This is different from the Santa Eleña Canyon Overlook parking lot. You'll see the Río Grande flowing out of the mouth of the canyon and Terlingua Creek ahead of you. On the other side of the creek you'll see the steps leading up the cliff face and into the canyon.

7. CLOSED CANYON, BIG BEND RANCH STATE PARK

I just love Closed Canyon. Maybe my fondness for this unusual place along Farm Road 170 is because I first discovered it by accident long before the state park existed and long before it was marked, or maybe because it's just so different since it's one of the very few slot canyons in Texas.

What makes Closed Canyon interesting is in its name. The canyon itself leads from the scenic River Road to the river itself and as you walk deeper into it, its tall walls close in. You walk on a usually dry creek bed of sand and over smooth rock, walking in extreme shadow and abrupt sunlight. About

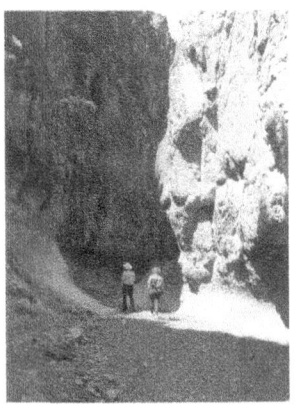

a half-mile in, the path drops and you have to scramble down, then it drops again, and again. After a while you reach a point where the drops are too steep for you to go any farther without the aid of ropes and friends who will remain behind to pull you back up. It's OK to stop when you arrive at a point too steep for you because by then you will have gotten the Closed Canyon experience.

The canyon is also called Cañon Obscuro because it can be quite dark inside even during midday.

Nothing about the walk is strenuous and it's not all that long, but look up at those sheer cliffs and notice a cactus here and there growing out of a spot of dirt lodged in a crack in the wall. This is a clear demonstration that life, even in the desert, is persistent. Stop and listen and you will certainly hear a hawk shrilling above you. Lean over into that cliff face and you'll discover long veins of calcite crystals.

This is another place where you need to be aware of the weather. The ground you're walking on is sandy because it's a dry creek bed that will flood in stormy weather and you don't want to be inside the canyon when that happens.

The trailhead is now easy to find since the state park has marked the canyon clearly from the road, and provided a large parking area and a trashcan. It's about 21 miles west of Lajitas on FM 170. Once you have parked, Closed Canyon is that obvious crack in the mesa wall you see south of you. Just walk toward it, then into it.

6. SOUTH RIM, BIG BEND NATIONAL PARK

The prize of this trail is sitting on the South Rim itself and seeing the vast Big Bend stretch out for miles and miles below you. On a clear day you can see deep into Mexico.

Although the South Rim itself is reason enough to take this hike, it also offers other attractions.

The trail goes up steeply in a series of switchbacks through the woods and eventually opens onto Laguna Meadow, a small valley with tall grasses and some juniper and pinyon pines.

At the South Rim itself you'll be perched on a steep escarpment, more than 2,500 feet above the foothills below you.

Boot Canyon is full of cypress, fir and maple trees, and Boot Spring is a refreshing stop along the way. This area is named for The Boot, a spire of volcanic rock that looks like an upside-down cowboy boot. Sorta. Relaxing at the spring you're bound to see one of the huge Mexican jays that hang out around here and perhaps even a rare Colima Warbler.

The only reason I don't rate this hike higher in this guide is because it's a strenuous ascent from 5,400 feet to 7,460 feet and because of its length—a 14-mile loop that is a true day hike only for the fit, especially if you want to spend any time seeing some of the spectacular sights along the way. And you should take the time. Most people take this hike now as a two-day backpacking trip. If you decide to do that, make certain to register with a ranger station first and pay attention to the limitations on where you can set up camp.

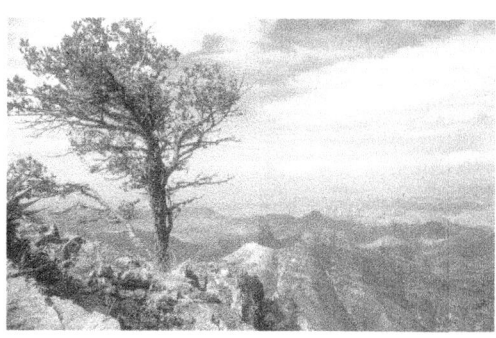

The trailhead is found at the big sign at the far end of the parking lot by the new lodges in the Basin, just to the west of the store.

5. GRAPEVINE HILLS, BIG BEND NATIONAL PARK

One of my favorite places, and one not seen by many visitors. The trail begins near the end of the 8-mile long Grapevine Hills dirt road. Some guides call this an improved dirt road, and it is just after it's been graded. But summer storms can make the road impassable in minutes, so consult with a ranger before traveling down it, and even then be prepared to encounter sandy or muddy conditions that will give a two-wheel drive vehicle fits.

The trail itself is an easy 2-mile roundtrip into a fascinating jumble of red rocks. Indian legend says that when God finished making the world, He tossed all the leftovers into the Big Bend. When you see the Grapevine Hills, you'll know how the legend got started. One of the most remarkable things to me about places like the Grapevine Hills is that even though it's technically visible from the paved road, you have no hint of what this place is like from that roadside viewpoint. I have to wonder: How many other spectacular places are hidden in plain sight if we just knew where to look?

A number of interesting formations can be seen along the way, but the best is a balanced rock that forms an arch. You have to scramble around to find it. Looking for it is easier these days since the park has put up small metal signs pointing in the correct direction; it's worth the effort. Photographic possibilities here are endless.

Be aware that it gets very hot here in the afternoon, and there is no water, so the best time to do this walk is before noon.

Just down the road from the hike is a campground that is my favorite in all the desert areas of the park.

The trailhead is located about seven miles down the Grapevine Hills Road. You'll see the parking area on your right.

4. THE WINDOW, BIG BEND NATIONAL PARK

A great half-day walk (5 miles round-trip) through the heart of the Chisos Basin along Oak Creek to the spot where most of the water in the Chisos flows down to the Chihuahuan Desert far below. This spot is called the

Window. Two cliffs form a distinctive V shape that is obvious from both inside the Basin and anywhere on the desert if you're facing east. However, the V doesn't actually connect at the base, it's an optical illusion created by the angle at which you're likely to see the hillsides.

The actual base is a rock slot just above the pour-off and only 20 feet wide. Be careful around this area, as all the rocks are very slippery. It's a long way down—220 feet.

Heading down to the window is a piece of cake. You descend about 800 feet through scrub brush then lush foliage along the banks of the creek. Chances are good you'll cross paths with a herd of javelina along the way down or back. Give them the right of way. If you're hiking in early morning or late afternoon, you also might see some whitetail deer roaming around. At one point before you get to the actual pour-off you will have to scramble through a slickrock canyon, through the creek and over some rocks. Be careful.

Another side trail—Oak Spring—heads off from the main trail near the pour-off. The first quarter-mile of it will take you to a scenic perch with far reaching views of the desert to the west.

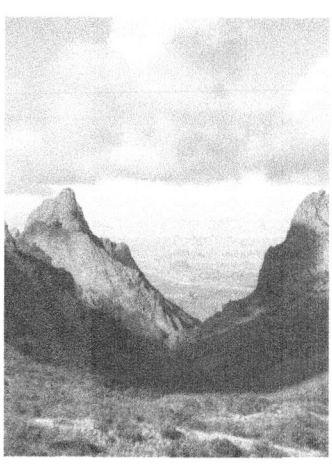

Remember that on the return hike you will have to hike back up those 800 feet you came down. That can be quite taxing when the weather is hot, so make certain you have more than enough water for the return trip.

One of the prizes when you're coming back is the sight of Casa Grande, one of the most distinctive landmarks in Big Bend. You'll have excellent views and photographic possibilities, especially when the big rock is framed by century plants or oaks or maples changing colors in the fall.

Do not confuse this trail with the quarter-mile Window View Trail that begins in the same area, offering perfect overlooks for sunsets through the Window. I confused the two once many years ago and ended up hiking the 2.5 miles back from the Window after dark (which, actually, was a nice experience).

The trailhead begins at the large sign at the far end of the parking lot by the new lodges in the Basin, just to the west of the store.

3. MULE EARS SPRING, BIG BEND NATIONAL PARK

This is a primitive, 4.5-mile roundtrip route without a well-maintained trail like you would find going to Lost Mine Peak or the Window. It's moderately strenuous, but gives you a good taste of what walking in the desert is all about. So it would not be recommended during the summer, since the trail is totally exposed to the sun. Mule Ears Peak may be the most distinctive landmark in Big Bend National Park, and once you see it you'll know how it got the name.

The formation is fairly complex geologically. Its base is an erosion-resistant basalt overlaid by tuff (hardened volcanic ash) then capped by lava dikes.

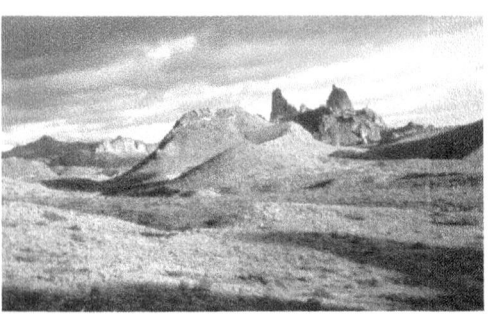

Over millennia, erosion worked its magic to get the peak into this shape. Wait another millennia or so and the Mule Ears may be leveled to their base.

When I call this an energetic option, please

believe me. One should be in good shape and carry plenty of water.

The hike itself offers you great views of the surrounding Sierra Quemada (Burned Mountains) and the huge wall of the Chisos Mountains.

Hikers are surprised, especially in hot weather, to discover a spring along with a corral and the ruins of an adobe house. It's nothing short of amazing to realize people lived and worked out here. Dip your tired feet in the cool spring and be refreshed.

You can also continue on from this point, scrambling around to keep heading toward the Mule Ears itself. It's a nice hike, but when it seems like the peak must be just around the next bend, it isn't. In fact, at the end of this very primitive trail you'll find yourself on a tall cliff edge overlooking the Smoky Creek Valley. This is a sight worth the walk, but it can be frustrating. To access Mule Ears Peak itself, a hiker must travel down the cliff, cross more desert, then climb up the base that forms the peak. To do all that you'll need another day and be in good shape.

The trail begins at the Mule Ears Overlook parking area along the Ross Maxwell Drive, abut 15 miles south from the main park road.

2. ERNST TINAJA, BIG BEND NATIONAL PARK

A great place to explore or relax. Max Ernst ran a post office and store here 100 years ago, before he was mysteriously murdered in 1908. The big tinaja named for him is in Ernst Canyon in the Dead Horse Mountains, about 4.5 miles north of the Río Grande Village Drive off the Old Ore Road. You drive to the canyon entrance, then walk about a half-mile in to the big tinaja where soldiers chasing Pancho Villa used to swim in their off hours.

As you wander deeper into the canyon, slow down and look down. This place is so full of subtle colors in the rock you'll be amazed: pastel blues, mauves, roses, tans, lavenders, yellows, and grays. The structures are multi-layered and get tilted wildly just up the canyon.

Linger at the big tinaja; it's the perfect place to lie back and relax. Then continue further into the canyon. Nearby, to your left, is a twisting rock chimney, an amazing and seemingly impossible work of nature that can be climbed through. Then wander up the canyon as far as you can.

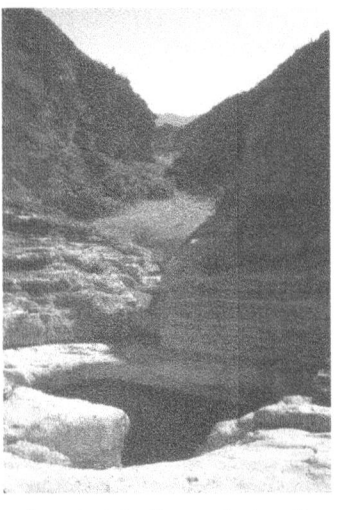

Climb around and enjoy yourself at one of the most refreshing, most unusual, and least accessible, places in the park.

The trailhead is located off the Old Ore Road, about 4.5 miles north from the main park road. You'll see small signs for the two campgrounds; turn at the second one that will take you into the parking area. The trail itself is not marked, so just follow the wash up into the canyon.

1. LOST MINE PEAK, BIG BEND NATIONAL PARK

This is one of the best hikes in the park to the second-best view in the park. It is a moderately strenuous, well-marked 5-mile round-trip trail up into the high Chisos Mountains. You can get a self-guiding booklet at the trailhead.

The trail starts at 5,600-feet elevation and goes up in a series of switchbacks to 6,850 feet, and it's a good trail to use a walking stick on. Most of the trail is through heavily wooded areas. That and the elevation usually keep the hike relatively cool. Among the trees you'll notice are several types of oak, juniper, sumac, ash, pine, and the only Mexican drooping juniper that grows in the United States. None is typical desert flora. And yet, you'll find them growing alongside desert plants like lechuguilla, ocotillo, sotol, and various types of cactus. That one tree you'll see that looks like it's suffering from a sunburn as it's red bark peels away to reveal a white skin is the Texas madrone.

The trail is initially quite steep but then levels out for a way. After a mile, you reach a saddle that looks over Juniper Canyon, up to Casa Grande, and into Mexico. After this, the trail gets steep again but ascends in a series of switchbacks that makes the going easier. Don't stop when you reach the top of the trail. Continue walking along the rock ridge to the very end where you'll see into Pine Canyon, over to the East Rim of the Chisos Mountains, and deep into Mexico.

The views along the trail are awesome, and the view from the end of the trail is like sitting on the edge of the world. On a clear day, you can see 100 miles from here.

Be aware that most mountain lion confrontations have occurred on this trail and on the South Rim Trail.

If you're wondering about the name, it stems from two versions of the same legend. Located somewhere near the summit is either the entrance to an old Spanish gold mine or a cave where legendary conquistador treasure was hidden. At a certain time of the year, if you stand at the door of the chapel of the Presidio San Vincente, 20 miles away in Mexico, you will see sunlight illuminate this entrance at sunrise. It is always possible that a treasure cave is hidden somewhere up here, but quite unlikely geologically that gold in any quantity is found. No one has ever found either.

The trailhead is well marked, along the road into the Chisos Basin just before it drops into the Basin.

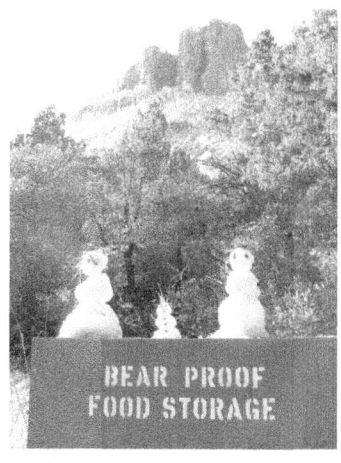

PART THREE
TOP ITINERARIES

The terrain and climate combine to render the Big Bend formidable to anyone traveling across it without reliable transportation. The terrain is rough, unpredictable, and hazardous. The desert is unyielding.
— Ronnie C. Tyler

Big Bend is nothing if not big. Depending on where you draw the imaginary boundary lines, the area is larger than many states. Big Bend National Park and Big Bend Ranch State Park are each about the size of Rhode Island, and that's not counting the huge areas outside of those parks. Such a large region, with so much to do and see within it, can leave a visitor quite confused. That's where these itineraries come in.

Each itinerary is a suggested guide for you to plan a trip of varying lengths. They aren't the last word, just suggestions for someone who has never been there by someone who is in his fifth decade of visiting. Feel free to mix and match from the options.

These suggestions are far from exhaustive — in fact, they just scratch the surface — and on subsequent trips to Big Bend you may want to discover new places. Included here are some of the best things about Big Bend.

Each place is rated with a star system, the more the better.
★★★★= You must see this place.
★★★ = Try hard to see this place.
★★ = See this place if you can.
★= If you've got the time, check this place out.

RIVER TRIPS

River trips are not included in every option since they are time consuming and highly dependent upon weather and river flow. Don't try to do a river trip on your own if you are not familiar with the river and don't have bona fide wilderness paddling experience. The isolated canyons of the Río Grande in the Big Bend aren't places to have problems. If you do get in trouble, you'll have great difficulty swimming or climbing out of the steep canyons; then face many miles of hiking to the closest road; and then you're still 100 miles from the nearest hospital.

However, if you have the time, and the river is flowing well and the weather isn't scorching, you should try to include a guided river trip in your plans. The Big Bend experience isn't quite the same without one. Some of the advantages of a guided trip are that the guide does all the work and you get history and geology lessons, too.

River trips can run anywhere from one day to several days. The most popular float is the two-day run through Santa Eleña Canyon; others include day trips through Colorado Canyon or Mariscal Canyon, or multiple-day trips through Boquillas Canyon and various combinations.

Spring (mid-February through April) offers you mild weather, a blooming desert and opportunities to see more wildlife, but the water levels are usually low. Summer (May through November) has the highest water flows, but the highest chance of rains. Winter (December through mid-February) is highly variable.

Also, at some point in the future, anyone doing a river trip is likely to be require to have a valid passport since the river is an international boundary. The U.S. government keeps postponing the date for this requirement, so ask an outfitter when you book your trip.

Many companies offer river trips, but the ones with the most experience on the Río Grande in the Big Bend are **Big Bend River Tours (432) 371-**

3033, Far Flung Outdoor Center (432) 371-2633, both in Study Butte, and Desert Sports (432) 371-2728 in Terlingua. Tell 'em the BIG BEND GUIDE sent you.

WHAT TO DO IN TWO DAYS
FORT DAVIS OPTION

Day One
Morning
✔ **Davis Mountains State Park.** ★★★ Here's a relaxing, scenic location, and a good place to begin or end any Big Bend trip. Located at the northern reaches of the Big Bend area in the Davis Mountains about three miles north of the city of Fort Davis on Texas 118, its 1,869 acres offers shaded campsites, hiking trails, a scenic drive, abundant wildlife, a decent restaurant, and a great hotel with pool. The Indian Lodge was built by the Civilian Conservation Corps during the Depression and has been expanded since. It features old-fashioned rooms—the original rooms have hand-crafted ceiling beams and furniture. The rooms are few and the prices low, so make reservations well in advance.

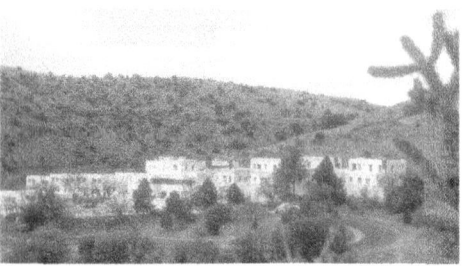

One hiking trail goes over a mountain to Fort Davis National Historical Park, offering unique, panoramic views. It can be done in its full 4.5-mile version from the Interpretive Center or a relatively short route from the Scenic Overlook near the Stone Tower at the end of the Scenic Drive.

Call (432) 426-3337 for more information on the park.

Call (432) 426-3254 for Indian Lodge reservations.

Afternoon

✔ **Fort Davis National Historical Park.** ★★★ This may be the best restored Western army post in the country, and to walk its parade ground and view its buildings is to step back in time more than 100 years. The enlisted barracks, complete with all the uniforms and equipment of a typical army frontier platoon all ready for inspection is worth the price of admission alone. And the fully furnished officers' quarters is quite a sight as well.

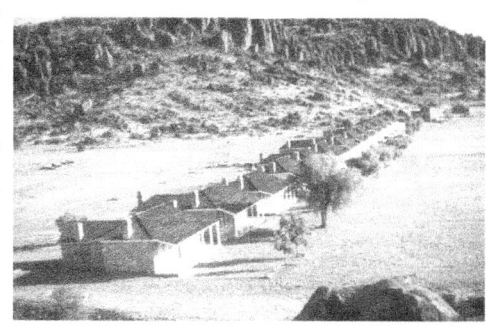

The Limpia Canyon location served as an army fort from 1854 to 1891, except during the Civil War. Soldiers from Fort Davis escorted stagecoaches, guarded mail relay stations, policed the Mexican border, fought Comanche and Apache warriors, and played a major role in driving Apache chief Victorio from Texas, ending Indian warfare in the state. Famous Civil War and Indian Wars Col. Benjamin Grierson once commanded the post.

Walk around ruins and restored buildings, hike into the cliffs and take your picture there like the officers did in the 1880s, listen to bugle calls wafting on the wind, visit the interpretive center and book store. This is what it was like in those days.

Call (432) 426-3224 for more information.

✔ **McDonald Observatory.** ★★★ Getting to the observatory is half the fun. It's only 17 miles from Fort Davis, but the 74-mile scenic loop on Texas 118 and 166 that cuts through the Davis Mountains is the highest highway in the state and one of the most beautiful.

The University of Texas operates McDonald Observatory, one of the best in the country thanks to the super dark West Texas skies and some of the biggest telescopes found anywhere. And the view from the top of the hill looking down on the Davis Mountains ain't bad either.

The largest telescopes in operation are the 362-inch telescope on 6,600-foot Mount Fowlkes, and the 107-inch and 82-inch big eyes on 6,800-foot Mount Locke.

The observatory hosts astronomers from around the world. You can take advantage of self-guided tours or one of the two daily guided tours. And if you'd like a stunning look at the sun, a telescope equipped with a safe filter and camera provides dramatic views of its many features also twice a day.

McDonald's evening Star Parties should not be missed. Beginning after sunset, several staff members lead visitors on a telescopic tour through the skies of stars, planets, and other astronomical objects.

The only reason I don't rate this stop higher is that not everyone is interested in astronomy. For those who are, it's a must-see.

The observatory also has a new interpretive center with a multimedia theater, public lectures, and many interactive exhibits perfect for kids.

Call (432) 426-3640 for more information.

Day Two
Morning
✔ **Drive to Big Bend National Park via Texas Highway 118.** ★★ My favorite route to Big Bend is U.S. Highway 67, but that's the long way around from Fort Davis. Texas 118 is pretty good, though. Take time to notice how the landscape changes, from the mountains of Fort Davis and Alpine, to the open desert with its mesas as you travel south, then the mountains again once you approach Study Butte. Most of the prominent peaks on both sides of the highway are marked with roadside signs that also note their elevation. Take your time and enjoy the drive. And wave back to passing motorists.

✔ **Down Old Maverick Drive (if open) and return Ross Maxwell Drive.** ★★★★

This may be the best, relatively quick introduction to the national park. Both routes lead to the mouth of Santa Eleña Canyon where there is, if you have time, a nice walk up the cliff on the American side and into the canyon (see Top Hike 8).

Old Maverick Drive isn't always open. It's an easy 14-mile gravel road, but sometimes it's washed out. The gate will be closed if the road is closed. Don't drive around it. The road passes through mostly barren landscape, including the Alamo Creek badlands. One stop you must make is Luna's Jacal, a dugout by the side of the road where Gilberto Luna raised dozens of children and even more goats until his death at 108. Note how small the jacal is, and how isolated it is, then feel the desert heat; that will make you appreciate the determination of early Big Bend settlers, a place even Indians didn't like to hang around much.

Near Santa Eleña Canyon is Terlingua Abaja, the ruins of an old farming community, and some backcountry camp-sites. Most of the ruins lie across Terlingua Creek, so you might get your feet wet.

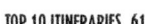

If you don't hike into the canyon, at least stop at the overlook. In the early morning, the mouth of the canyon, with its sheer cliffs on both sides, can be spectacular. Note how green it is along the Río Grande, compared to the countryside you just drove through.

The Ross Maxwell Drive is a 30-mile paved road returning to the main park highway from Santa Eleña Canyon and is dotted with several places you'll want to stop at and explore.

Among the sights are several ruins that can't be seen from the road. Watch for the signs, pull off at the parking area and walk to the sites. If you hap-

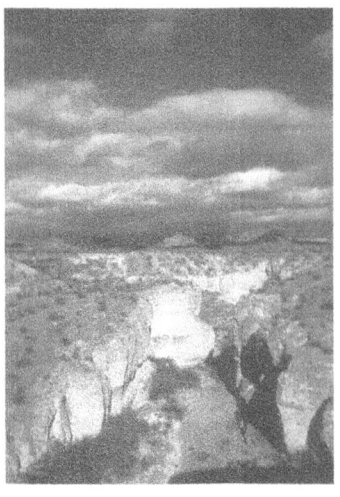

pen to be out during the summer, you'll find it difficult to believe people lived here in these adobe shacks.

Other attractions along the road are Sotol Vista, with its commanding view of the south of the park and into Mexico, Burro Mesa Pouroff with its waterfall in wetter weather, Castolon and Cerro Castellan, Tuff Canyon, and the Mule Ears Peak overlook. Cottonwood Campground is also along this road.

NOTE: The crossing into the village of Santa Heleña, Mexico, is also along this road but the Office of Homeland Security closed all of the unofficial crossings—such as Boquillas, Santa Heleña, and Paso Lajitas—in and around the park in 2002. If you cross, you face serious fines and possible jail time if apprehended on your return. The Boquillas crossing, however, has now reopened. It uses an unusual video kiosk to scan passports. Buy tickets at the Rio Grande Store, return to the customs office along the main park road, walk down to the river behind the office and take a boat across the Rio Grande at the crossing. It's a very small village but is home to a bar, restaurant, gift shop, small motel, and some great views upriver. The nearest major official crossing, which you may drive across, is at Presidio into Ojinaga, about 100 miles west of the national park.

Afternoon
✔ **Snack at Castolon.** ★★ A self-guided tour of ruins of this old farming settlement is a central feature here, along with the store. The trading post is just as it was around the turn of the century and is a favorite stop for tourists who seek some ice cream and a shady place to relax. Picnic tables

cluster under a ramada at the front of the store.

You can see Cerro Castellan from here, just a ways up the road. The peak is, along with Mule Ears, one of the most distinctive landmarks in Big Bend. Sometimes, the setting sun will light up the peak as if the rock was made of gold.

Explore the area around the peak, treading on black basalt and white tuff on both sides of the road. You may find a large rocky hill with a window-size hole through it.

✔ **Lost Mine Peak Trail. ★★★★** One of the best hikes in the park to the second best view in the park (see Top Hike 1). Be aware that most mountain lion confrontations have occurred on this trail and on the South Rim Trail.

✔ **Dinner at Chisos Mountain Lodge. ★★★** This gets its high rating not for the food at the restaurant, which is fine, but from the view. All the tables look out onto the Window, a V formation created by the sides of the Chisos Basin that frames the desert to the west below. Sunsets through the Window can be very memorable. You'll likely see some wildlife, too. I've seen everything from beautiful birds, chattering squirrels, ugly javelina, and bear.

The mountain directly behind the restaurant is Casa Grande, perhaps the trademark formation of Big Bend National Park. The big hill directly in front of the eatery is Appetite Hill, where more youthful visitors, usually scout groups, climb around before dinner.

✔ **Ranger Talk.**

(Rating depends on talk and the ranger giving it.) Rangers give a number of interpretive programs, many of them quite interesting, at different locations in the park. There is almost always one in the early evening at the Basin Amphitheater that makes for a nice after-dinner treat. You can check schedules and topics on a list at the visitor center, ranger stations and campground bulletin boards.

EL CAMINO RÍO OPTION

Day One
Morning

✔ **Drive to Presidio on U.S. 67. ★★★** My favorite route into Big Bend, U.S. 67, traverses some very empty, although hilly, landscapes. You'll find almost nothing on the 60-mile road from Marfa to Presidio, and that's what makes it interesting. Other than the paved road itself, any travelers from 100 years ago would easily recognize this place. Can't say that about Houston or Boston.

One interesting stop is the ghost town of Shafter. Check out the cemetery and the old mine. Although Shafter is a ghost town, a few people still insist on living here. There's even a church. Sometimes there is a store or gas station or restaurant open here. More often, there's not. Don't depend on any.

Lt. Col. William Shafter began a silver mine here in 1880. By the time it closed in 1942, more than $20 million worth of silver had been torn from the land. Today, the old mining area looks like a bomb site, and walking around can be quite treacherous.

Usually old silver towns capture the popular imagination, but most travelers to the Big Bend aren't even aware of Shafter's glittering history. Maybe because it's so remote.

Nearby is a rock formation, noted with a highway sign, that looks like Abe Lincoln's profile. One of the few formations that actually lives up to its billing.

At the end of the road is Presidio, where a bridge will take you into Mexico. Unfortunately, Presidio isn't much to see for a typical tourist. For real bargains on items like high-quality liquors and name-brand jewelery, check out the duty-free shop on the American side, located near the spur road that leads to the international bridge.

Presidio's Mexican companion Ojinaga is a little better, but is unlike other border cities such as Acuña or Matamoros or Juárez. It's a generally quiet place, more Mexican than Texican. Most of the action and shops are along the main street and prices are cheap. To return to the United States from Mexico you now need a valid passport or passport card.

If you're feeling adventurous and have some spare time, there's an alternate route off U.S. 67 that will take you to Farm Road 170. It's marked on maps as Ranch Road 169 and is paved for a few miles. The improved dirt road travels across working ranches and through the most desolate country you will find here. You'll cross a number of cattle guards because the road traverses several private ranches. Stay on the road; don't trespass. The road follows the Old Chihuahua Trail that one time was the major trading route between the cities of Chihuahua and San Antonio. Ox carts from Fort Leaton were a familiar sight here. The road ends near Fort Leaton on Farm Road 170.

Check out what little is left of the abandoned train depot at Plata, about midway.

Near the end of this route, one road turns off to the left and on into Big Bend Ranch State Park.

Call the Presidio Information Center at (432) 229-4478.

Call Big Bend Ranch State Park at (432) 229-3416.

✔ **Fort Leaton State Historical Site.** ★★★★ The state has just about completed restoration of this one-acre large, private adobe fortress that served as home and trading post through the middle to late 1800s. The walls are as much as 2 feet thick, cooling the inside considerably even in the worst summer heat. Some rooms have fireplaces large enough to cook an entire side of beef. This is a place with a particularly bloody history. To learn more, get a copy of my book on the fort (see Appendix A)—it's a historical novel, but it's the only book that exists on this unusual place. You can also get more information on and permits for Big Bend Ranch State Park here.

Call (432) 229-3613.

✔ **Drive to Lajitas on Farm Road 170.** ★★★

The River Road is billed as one of the most scenic drives in the United States and pretty much lives up to its reputation. For most of the distance between Presidio and Lajitas, the road follows the Río Grande where it becomes very obvious some international boundaries are nothing more than imaginary lines. You won't see much difference on either side of the river.

About two miles east of the small community of Redford, look for a tall, ugly rock formation known as the Goblin on the north side of the highway. You'll see a dirt road leading to it, drive in and park. The "ruins" you see here are a movie set built for the *Lonesome Dove* sequel *Streets of Laredo*. But the area is far more interesting for its rock formations, like the Goblin, and one that looks like a huge tortoise, and all the small caves eroded into the surrounding cliff faces.

Don't miss the unmarked overlook at the top of Big Hill (don't worry, you'll know when you get there, the hill is steep enough that RVs will wheeze going up its 15 percent grade.) For a classic view of Big Bend and the river, look upriver. If you're a fan of the Kevin Costner film *Fandango*, wander around the rocks to look for one with the word "DOM" carved on it that was used in the movie (hint: it's on the downriver side). You have to see the movie to understand what "DOM" means; I'm not tattling.

Another roadside parking area not far away overlooks The Hoo Doos, odd shaped rock formations on the side of the river. The Hoo Doos south of the highway, are part of the state park and are marked with a small sign and a new parking area.

You'll notice what looks like an old ruin on the south side of the highway.

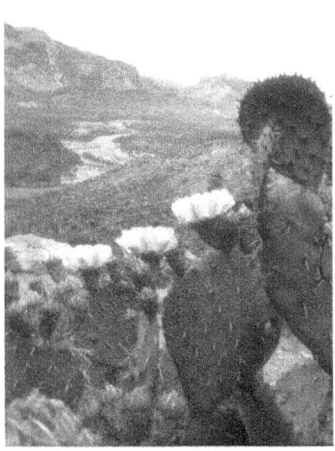

This is the Contrabando Movie Set where they filmed *Uphill All the Way* and *The Journeyman*, along with the TV mini-series *Streets of Laredo* and *Dead Man's Walk*. The site once had many buildings, including a scenic church, but Texas Parks and Wildlife Department deemed them to be a hazard and they were demolished. Only the original building remains; look around and inside to see how Hollywood creates its magic. The site also has an outhouse so you can squat where James Garner once answered Nature's summons. Because the Rio Grande here is so shallow and narrow you might be tempted to tiptoe to the Mexican side—don't. It's illegal and you'll face significant fines if caught.

✔ **Closed Canyon/Cañon Obscuro.** ★★★ A nice canyon on the south side of the road, this is a leisurely walk (less than a mile) into the heart of an unusual desert canyon. The canyon, now part of Big Bend Ranch State Park, is quite narrow with steep walls, so it's usually cool, even dark in some places. After rains the rocks can be slick, so watch out. The canyon ultimately leads to the river, but you can't get all the way without ropes and other climbing gear (see Top Hike 7).

At one point on the highway you'll notice a wall of white rock on the north side of the road. This is all volcanic ash and it's quite crumbly, so don't climb up on it. One visitor climbed up on one of its unusual formations, El Padre al Altar/the Priest at the Altar, and this unusual display has now collapsed.

And if you're looking for a pleasant place to have a snack or picnic lunch, pull over at the Tee Pees rest stop and take advantage of the shade from the faux tee pees.

Afternoon

✔ **Lajitas.** ★★ No one is really certain how long the community of Lajitas has been around. Comanches used the crossing here as a ford into Mexico on their annual raids. An archaeological site of an old Comanche camp along nearby Comanche Creek has been discovered and partially detailed.

Some settlers lived here in the 1880s. After the turn of the century, Gen. John J. Pershing established a cavalry post on the spot while chasing Pancho Villa through northern Mexico. One of the modern motel units is built on the ruins of that old post. It's said Villa himself shopped often at the Trading Post, which is now closed.

By the 1960s, Lajitas was just the Trading Post, a house by the store, and a couple of shacks. Today it is a full-fledged resort town. You will also find a restored mission church that still conducts services and an old cemetery by the north side of the road.

✔ **Barton Warnock Environmental Education Center.** ★★★ Originally built by the resort to showcase the Lajitas area, it was taken over by the state of Texas when it acquired Big Bend Ranch a few years back and is now part of the state park. This is a worthwhile museum, highlighting the cultural and natural history of the area, with an interesting desert garden out back featuring just about every plant you're likely to encounter out here. My favorite display is the gigantic pterosaur skeleton. You can also get more information on and permits for Big Bend Ranch State Park here. It's located on Farm Road 170 just east of Lajitas. Call (432) 424-3327.

✔ **Terlingua Ghost Town.** ★★★ At least three specific places are called Terlingua in Big Bend (see Appendix C), but the best known is the area around Terlingua Creek on Farm Road 170.

For many years, Terlingua was a thriving mining town, digging cinnabar out of the ground and refining it into quicksilver, or mercury. The big house you see on a hill behind the town is the Perry Mansion, built by Howard Perry, owner of the Chisos Mining Company, for his new bride. Legend has it that Mrs. Perry traveled from the northeast to Terlingua, took one look around and headed back home. The mansion was abandoned and today is in danger of falling down. A couple of rooms in the mansion have been restored and you can now spend the night there. Check with the folks at the Terlingua Trading Company on the boardwalk in town.

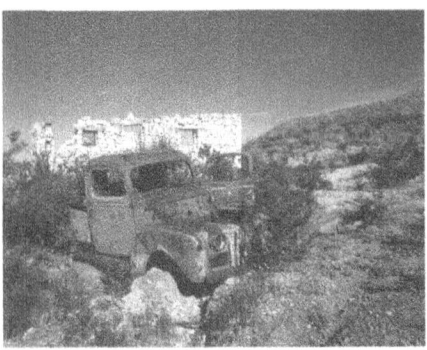

The area that locals call the Ghost Town is actually quite populated now. You'll notice ruins all over the hills, remnants of that old quicksilver mine and the people who ran it. You'll find a brochure for a self-guided tour of the mine at the **Terlingua Trading Company**, a huge gift shop and bookstore, the best in the area, with fine jewelry, Mexican crafts, and chili stuff. People, usually river guides, have renovated some of these jacals and live in them so don't just go wandering in any. One area of ruins to the east of the Ghost Town has been used in a couple of films, notably Willie Nelson's *Barbarosa* and *Streets of Laredo*, based on the Larry McMurtry novel.

Just before town, on the spur road from Farm Road 170, is a cemetery that offers some good photographic possibilities at sunrise and dusk. The other dirt roads lead to homes in the hills north of Terlingua and, in many cases, the folks who live out in those remote areas do so because they don't like company, so respect their privacy.

Terlingua Ghost Town proper has restaurants, a motel, the gift shop, and an art gallery.

Terlingua is best known for the annual world championship chili cook-off. Now there are two of them, neither exactly in Terlingua.

The chili crown has been determined here since 1967. About 20 years ago, the main chili heads split into two groups: the more traditional group, then led by cook-off founder Frank X. Tolbert and currently run by his daughter Kathleen, meets behind the **Terlingua Store** to the south of Farm Road 170. It's called, originally enough, the Behind the Store chili championship. The larger, more commercial group, meets just west of the Ghost Town to the north of FM 170. You'll see the big CASI (Chili Appreciation Society International) sign. Both championships are held the first weekend in November, and lodging and campsites are booked a year in advance all through Big Bend. For information on the two cook-offs, visit the Web sites listed in Appendix D.

Be aware that on chili weekend, state troopers love to lie in wait along Texas 118 and FM 170 and just reel in speeders and drunk drivers as fast as they can write tickets.

✔ **Cocktails at La Kiva.** ★★ Located at the Big Bend Travel Park, just over the Terlingua bridge on Farm Road 170, this is a unique Big Bend experience. You don't just enter La Kiva, you descend into it after opening an enormous door balanced on counter weights. The bar and restaurant is built into the ground, and the decor is dark and quite eclectic. The bar is a favorite hangout of colorful local residents. Call (432) 371-2250.

✔ **Dinner at Starlight Theatre.** ★★★★ As of this writing, the Starlight has the best food within 300 miles, maybe more. It boasts a huge mesquite bar and a cowboy campfire mural by Stylle Read along the back wall. The bar scene now rivals La Kiva's for colorful locals. The Starlight features live musical entertainment on many nights, usually weekends and holidays.

When mining was booming, this was a movie house. In 1986, Big Bend was one of the few places you could see Halley's Comet clearly on one of its rare return trips and one Spring evening Texas troubadour Jerry Jeff Walker held an impromptu concert for about 20 people in the building that was missing a back wall and a ceiling. His concert under the stars gave the old theater its new name. In 1991, the ruin was renovated and opened as the

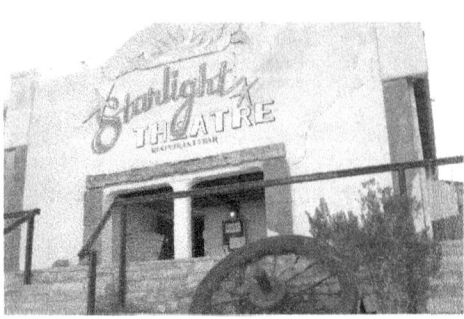

Starlight restaurant. If you look at the wall behind you as you come in, you'll notice a great folk sculpture of a comet.

If you're around just before sundown, join the locals on the long bench on the porch between the **Terlingua Trading Company** store and the **Starlight**. Ask and they'll all have a story to tell. You'll also notice near-ly all are nursing six packs of beer and facing east. If you ask what they're doing, some will tell you, honestly, they're waiting for the sunset. If you think the brews have gone to their heads, just wait around because on a good day the setting sun can reflect glorious colors off the Chisos Mountains to the east of you. And if it's a full moon evening, you'll be treated double as that silvery orb rises near Casa Grande and puts on a show of its own. (For stories from the Terlingua Porch, see *Appendix A*.) Call (432) 371-2326.

Day Two
Morning

✔ **Orientation at Panther Junction HQ.** ★★★ Pay your entry fee to Big Bend National Park at the Maverick entrance at the end of Texas 118, then take a leisurely drive to park headquarters at Panther Junction. Once there, you can check on weather reports, on driving conditions for the various roads in the park, and what special activities and talks are being offered.

In the middle of the lobby is a giant three-dimensional map of the park. For sale are posters and slides and DVDs, along with many good books about the Big Bend area, deserts, parks, wildlife, plants, and geology. Even coloring books for kids. Next door is a post office.

The best part of the headquarters for a first-time visitor, however, is outside in the desert garden. This is a self-guided, quarter-mile walk past just about every plant that grows in the Big Bend, familiarizing you with what you've been seeing and will be seeing in your travels. The accompanying brochure explains all about each one. Call (432) 477-2251 for more information about Big Bend National Park.

✔ **Hot Springs/Ojo Caliente.** ★★★ Hot Springs used to be a bustling little place. J.O. Langford ran a health resort here, and Maggie Smith's post office was the center of social life for miles around on both sides of the river. They are preserved, along with what is left of the bathhouse that Langford built over the spring that bubbles up many degrees warmer than the surrounding Río Grande.

Scientists say the 105-degree spring is water from millions of years ago that is not being replenished, so at some future point in time it will cease to flow.

Along the walk from the old post office to the hot spring are several ancient petroglyphs and pictographs (look high) and hundreds of cliff swallow mud nests (look higher).

Be aware that this can be a very hot place, especially in summer. Even on the easy 1-mile walk along the river to the hot spring, you should be drinking lots of water.

The road to Hot Springs is marked along the main park road. Follow the dirt spur to a parking area and follow the signs to the spring.

Afternoon
- ✔ **Lost Mine Peak Trail** (*Top Hike 1*)
- ✔ **Dinner at Chisos Mountain Lodge**
- ✔ **Ranger talk**

BIG BEND RANCH STATE PARK OPTION

Day One
Morning
- ✔ **Fort Leaton State Historic Site**
- ✔ **Big Bend Ranch State Park Drive.** ★★★

The largest of Texas state parks, at 400 square-mile size. It was a working cattle ranch, and a small herd of longhorns remains. Much of this park remains closed to visitors, unless you want to hike on the 20-mile long, challenging Rancherías Trail that should be tried by experienced backpackers only.

Recently, more of the park was opened and several relatively short hike and/or bike trails have been marked. More are set to open.

Some of the park lies along Farm Road 170, but the heart of the park is in a rugged wilderness between Redford and Presidio, well north of the river. To find it, turn north on the Casa Piedra Road just east of Fort Leaton. Turn right off this 7-mile gravel road when you see the sign for the park. Then you have another 20 miles (approximately) on another rough but passable gravel road to the Visitors Center at La Sauceda. Make certain you pay your entry fee at either Fort Leaton near Presidio or the Warnock Center in Lajitas to get a map for the park. Along the drive, you'll see unusual rock formations, typical desert plants and animals, and even one prehistoric Indian shelter alongside the road and some pictographs if you know where to look (hint: ask a ranger when you pay your entry fee or at the Visitor Center).

The Solitario/Fresno Canyon overlook is near the end of the road, another 6 miles (approximately), and worth the drive. The Solitario is a massive circular formation only completely visible from the air. It spewed out magma and was almost a volcano, but collapsed and didn't quite make the grade. The area is terribly rugged and until recently was seen by only a handful of dedicated hunters in the pre-park days and four-wheelers.

Several primitive campsites are available, as well as bunkhouse-style accommodations and private rooms at La Sauceda. Unless you have a four-wheel-drive vehicle, much of what little else is open will not be passable. However, access to areas in the state park is growing and several hiking and biking trails are now open. Because just driving around in this area takes up much of your time, if you're planning on doing any of the trails you should stay in the park or in nearby Presidio to make a two- or three-day stay of it.

Because of the time you'll need for this drive, if you haven't had a picnic lunch along the way, drive up to Presidio and have lunch at The Patio restaurant when you're back out of the park. Call (432) 229-3416.

Afternoon
- ✔ **Closed Canyon** (*Top Hike 7*)
- ✔ **Dinner at Lajitas**

Day Two
Morning
- ✔ **Orientation at Panther Junction HQ**
- ✔ **Ernst Tinaja** (*Top Hike 2*)

Afternoon
- ✔ **Lost Mine Peak Trail** (*Top Hike 1*)
- ✔ **Dinner at Chisos Mountain Lodge**
- ✔ **Ranger Talk**

BIG BEND NATIONAL PARK OPTION 1 (*Moderate*)

Day One
Morning
- ✔ **Orientation at Panther Junction HQ**
- ✔ **Down Old Maverick Road**
- ✔ **Up Ross Maxwell Drive**
- ✔ **Lunch at Castolon**

Afternoon
- ✔ **Window Trail** (*Top Hike 4*)

✔ **Dinner at Chisos Mountain Lodge.**
✔ **Ranger Talk**

Day Two
Morning

✔ **Hot Springs**
✔ **Boquillas Canyon Trail.** ★★ Boquillas Canyon is the easternmost of the three steep canyons along the Río Grande within the national park and the longest at 25 miles. River runners who begin from here are usually on a multi-day trip because so few take-out opportunities exist downstream. In addition, once it leaves the park the river flows for many miles in primitive territory, many miles from the nearest road so such a trip should not be attempted by amateurs. The usual takeout at La Linda is 30 miles away.

But you can walk for some distance into the canyon. It's about a mile and a half roundtrip, and it's much easier than the walk into Santa Eleña Canyon but because the head of the Boquillas Canyon is much wider than the mouth at Santa Eleña, the surroundings aren't nearly as dramatic. You are, however, walking over fossil-encrusted limestone more than 100 million years old. When the trail drops into the canyon look for two things, one obvious and one not so obvious. The first is the huge sand dune on the American side just below a shallow cave. Kids love trudging up the dune then sliding or rolling down it. The second thing to look for is a collection of metates, mortar holes that Indians used to grind mesquite beans or grains in to make flour for breads.

Afternoon

✔ **Lost Mine Peak Trail** (*Top Hike 1*)
✔ **Cookout or Dinner at Chisos Mountain Lodge**
✔ **Ranger Talk**

BIG BEND NATIONAL PARK OPTION 2 (*Energetic*)

Day One
Morning

✔ **Orientation at Panther Junction HQ**
✔ **Mule Ears Spring Trail** (Top Hike 3). This route gives you a good

taste of what walking in the desert is all about and when I call this an energetic option, please believe me and be in good shape and carry lots of water.

Afternoon
- ✔ **Lost Mine Peak Trail** *(Top Hike 1)*
- ✔ **Cookout or Dinner at Chisos Mountain Lodge**
- ✔ **Ranger Talk**

Day Two
Morning
- ✔ **Grapevine Hills** *(Top Hike 5)*

Afternoon
- ✔ **Window Trail** *(Top Hike 4)*
- ✔ **Dinner at Chisos Mountain Lodge**
- ✔ **Ranger Talk**

WHAT TO DO IN FIVE DAYS
ALPINE/FORT DAVIS/MARFA OPTION

Day One
Morning
✔ **Davis Mountains State Park**
Afternoon
✔ **Scenic Loop Drive**
✔ **McDonald Observatory**
✔ **Marfa.** ★ Marfa is the seat of Presidio County and has a nice, large courthouse that it seems still a little out of place for such a small town, even one that's been "discovered" by art fans who are turning it into a sort of mini-Santa Fe. You can climb the stairs to a lookout at the top of the courthouse for a great view of the countryside.

Check out the town's new art galleries and bookshop, Marfa Books, which has a monumental selection of hefty art books as well as a superb espresso bar where colorful locals gather every morning.

Don't forget to gas up before you head south.

✔ **Giant.** ★ Marfa's main claim to fame is that the movie *Giant* was made near here in 1955. That site, on a private ranch, used to be open but is closed now. Not much left but the crumbled façade of Reata anyway. The Paisano Hotel downtown, where some of the actors bunked, has a display about the making of the film.

✔ **The Chinati Foundation.** ★★ This place, just south of town at old Fort D.A. Russell off U.S. 67, enjoys an international reputation as an art space, featuring several renowned artists that draws visitors from near and far. But you'll have to decide for yourself whether the stark metal cubes by the late sculptor Donald Judd set in empty military buildings constitute great art or a great con job. Call (432) 729-4362 for information on the Chinati Foundation.

✔ **Marfa Lights.** ★★★ Everybody wants to see the famous Marfa Lights, but the lights are fickle: Sometimes the magic works and sometimes it doesn't. The viewing location is at a roadside park nine miles east of Marfa on U.S. 90. You'll almost never be alone there, even in coldest winter. The lights kind of dance or float in the distance, on the plain in front of the far mountains, and they're quite eerie.

Several stories surround the lights. Some say they are ghosts of dead prospectors or Indians, others say it's ignited gases, others claim its jackrabbits that have run through phosphorescent bushes, while skeptics insist they are merely reflections from oncoming vehicles.

There's no question that some of the lights you see are headlight reflections or refractions, but the trouble with this facile explanation is that the lights have been observed since the 1800s when no motor vehicles were around. I'm signing on to the jackrabbit theory. Check 'em out and make your own decision.

Call the local chamber of commerce at (432) 729-4942 for more information on Marfa and the Marfa Lights.

✔ Drive to Fort Davis.

Along Texas Highway 17 to Fort Davis you may spot a small blimp in the sky. That's the Border Patrol's aerostat, a radar-equipped device searching for aircraft, usually carrying illicit drugs, entering the U.S. illegally. And keep an eye out for the pronghorn antelope that range in these parts. Dine and stay in Fort Davis.

Day Two

Morning

✔ Overland Trail Museum. ★★ If you walk around Fort Davis much, you'll notice some deep ruts in the ground. These were carved by years of use by wagons and stages on the Overland Trail, and this museum near the restored fort preserves those memories and others about the city Fort Davis. Once privately operated and only sporadically open, the museum is now run by the Fort Davis Historical Society and has regular hours in the afternoons. Call (432) 426-2467.

✔ Fort Davis National Historic Site.

Afternoon

✔ Chihuahuan Desert Research Institute. ★★★ Just south of Fort

Davis toward Alpine, the institute has one of the world's largest collections of cactus and other desert plants. There's even a self-guided hike to a hidden spring. Call (432) 364-2499.

✔ **Alpine.** ★★★ Alpine isn't what you might expect. Surrounded by mountains at an elevation of 4,481 feet, it's a real oasis in the upper Chihuahuan Desert. The city grew up around a spring first called Alsate's Spring, later known as Burgess Waterhole, and then Kokernot Springs. It is now home to Sul Ross University, one of the few colleges in the country where you can major in rodeo.

Several hotels offer accommodations in town. Alpine is the best place to stock up on groceries, since it has two large supermarkets with just about anything you could need. And don't forget to gas up before heading south.

The city plays host to the annual Texas Cowboy Poetry Gathering in March, and is a wonderful entertainment if you can plan your trip to include it. Sul Ross hosts an intercollegiate rodeo in October.

Call the Alpine chamber at (432) 837-2326 for information on lodging. The city has several fast food restaurants, along with Italian food at La Trattoria that will fill up good and proper and the Reata, offering gourmet cowboy cuisine.

✔ **The Stable** ★★ You may have expected to find a stable of ponies in this Western town, but not a Stable full of Mustangs. Several world class Shelby Mustangs, no less. This performance car museum showcases a few dozen Shelbys, including the Terlingua Racing Team's V6 Mustang that celebrates the original chili cook-off. A gift shop features everything you could imagine in Shelby apparel and souvenirs. The museum also hosts several events throughout the year. Call 432 (837) 9789.

✔ **Museum of the Big Bend.** ★★★ A good place to get introduced to the Big Bend. The newly renovated museum is in a historic house on the campus of Sul Ross University, has a small gift shop, and a large museum housing artifacts from the area's history. One impressive sight is an old stagecoach full of bullet holes. Call (432) 837-8143.

Day Three
Morning
- ✔ To Marfa, then Presidio
- ✔ Fort Leaton State Historic Site
- ✔ Lunch at El Patio

Afternoon
- ✔ Farm Road 170
- ✔ Closed Canyon *(Top Hike 7)*
- ✔ Dinner at Starlight Restaurant
- ✔ Dinner at Lajitas

Day Four
Morning
- ✔ Orientation at Panther Junction HQ
- ✔ Down Old Maverick Road
- ✔ Up Ross Maxwell Drive
- ✔ Lunch at Castolon

Afternoon
- ✔ Window Trail *(Top Hike 4)*
- ✔ Dinner at Chisos Mountain Lodge
- ✔ Ranger Talk

Day Five
Morning
- ✔ Grapevine Hills *(Top Hike 5)*

Afternoon
- ✔ Lost Mine Peak Trail *(Top Hike 1)*
- ✔ Dinner at Chisos Mountain Lodge
- ✔ Ranger Talk

BIG BEND NATIONAL PARK OPTION

Day One
Morning
- ✔ Fort Leaton State Historic Site
- ✔ Farm Road 170

   ✔ **Closed Canyon** *(Top Hike 7)*

Afternoon
   ✔ **Terlingua Ghost Town**
   ✔ **Dinner at Starlight Dinner Theater**

Day Two.
   ✔ **Orientation at Panther Junction HQ**
   ✔ **Down Old Maverick Road**
   ✔ **Up Ross Maxwell Drive**
   ✔ **Santa Eleña Canyon Trail** *(Top Hike 8)*
   ✔ **Burro Mesa Pour-off.** ★★ An easy 1-mile round trip that can be quite hot in the summer. The trail begins at a marked point on the Burro Mesa spur road off the Ross Maxwell Drive, leading you into a classic box canyon at the end of which is the pour-off. Water runs off Burro Mesa down the funnel it has carved into the face of the cliff and, if you're lucky and there has been a recent storm, you'll see a significant waterfall here and this becomes a three-star visit. Otherwise, the pour-off is marked by discoloration and deformation in the canyon wall. That's a 3.5-mile round trip, difficult primitive trail.
   ✔ **Castolon**
   ✔ **Cookout or Dinner at Chisos Mountain Lodge**
   ✔ **Ranger Talk**

Day Three
Morning
   ✔ **Grapevine Hills** *(Top Hike 5)*
   ✔ **Hot Springs**

Afternoon
   ✔ **Mule Ears Spring Trail** *(Top Hike 3)*
   ✔ **Cookout or Dinner at Chisos Mountain Lodge**
   ✔ **Ranger Talk**

Day Four
Morning
   ✔ **Lost Mine Peak Trail** *(Top Hike 1)*

Afternoon

✔ **Dagger Flats.** ★★★ This rating is contingent upon the time of the year. When the dagger yucca are blooming (March or early April, if there are sufficient winter rains) this vista is among the best in the park. Without those soft, white flowers topping off the towering plants, it's less so.

A 7.5-mile dirt road off the Persimmon Gap Drive takes you to Dagger Flats, home to hundreds of these giant yuccas, some as tall as 15 feet. Other than the beauty of their blooms and their impressive size, the dagger yuccas here are also interesting because you can only find them in the Chihuahuan Desert.

✔ **Río Grande Village Trail.** ★★ An easy loop walk of a little less than a mile, the trail passes through river vegetation that is almost like being in a jungle then up to the desert. An overlook offers a great view and photographic possibilities of the Río Grande and Mexico.

A similar experience is available on the Santa Eleña Canyon Trail at the opposite end of the park.

Río Grande Village itself has a gas station and small store, along with the only public washing machines and showers in the park.

✔ **Cookout or Dinner at Chisos Mountain Lodge**
✔ **Ranger Talk**

Day Five
Morning
✔ **Ernst Tinaja** *(Top Hike 2)*

Afternoon
✔ **Window Trail** *(Top Hike 4)*
✔ **Dinner at Chisos Mountain Lodge**
✔ **Ranger Talk**

BIG BEND NATIONAL PARK RIVER OPTION

Day One
Morning
✔ **Farm Road 170**
✔ **Lunch at Lajitas**
✔ **Orientation at Panther Junction HQ**

Afternoon
- ✔ **Hot Springs**
- ✔ **Boquillas Canyon**
- ✔ **Dinner at Chisos Mountain Lodge**

Day Two and Three
- ✔ **Santa Eleña Canyon Raft Trip ★★★★**

If weather and time permits, a guided trip through Santa Eleña Canyon is highly recommended. This is usually a two-day float beginning at the Lajitas ford and taking out just past the mouth of the canyon some 17 miles away. If you're an experienced wilderness paddler, arrange a shuttle from one of the outfitters in Study Butte or Terlingua, but remember to get a river permit first from the national park headquarters.

On the first day your guide will regale you with history and geology as you float leisurely through the desert along the international border that is the Río Grande and you will truly have the feeling that you are on the last

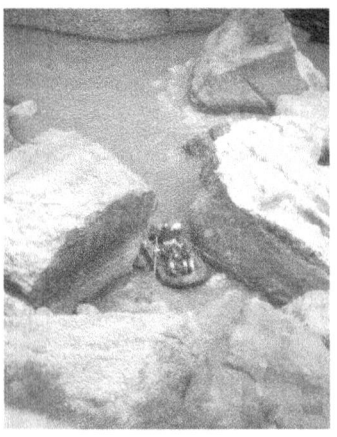

frontier. You camp out at the head of the canyon. While your guide is making dinner, walk a ways into the canyon, look up at the sheer walls that reach more than 1,500 feet in some places on both sides, and contemplate what you will go through the next day. It seems a mystery because the river makes a sharp turn here and you cannot see deeply into the canyon—all you see is the unknown—and recall that once you're in the canyon, there's no way out except through.

The second day your raft shifts between bright sunlight and deep shadows as the river bends this way and that on its 7-mile trip through the canyon. Quite soon you may feel as if you're in a cathedral, both because of the walls looming heavenward all around you and because the silence and natural beauty of this place inevitably lead to spiritual thoughts. Perhaps you'll stop for lunch at Fern Canyon. To get to this side canyon you have to swim just a little through a cool, emerald pool then climbing over some rocks to see polished limestone cliff walls in the narrow canyon covered in ferns growing from travertine springs.

If doing this trip on your own, be wary of the Rockslide, located about a mile inside the canyon. Over time, portions of the cliff walls have broken away and dropped into the river. Big portions. Whatever you do, get a map and know for certain where the Rockslide is located, then scout it on the American side before you attempt to run it. This is usually rated as very difficult, usually a Class IV. That rating isn't because it has any real rapids—this is more of a blind maze than a rapid—but because of the house-sized rock smack in the middle of the current, and so many other huge boulders that you can't see over and around. To make it through this area, you will have to perfectly execute turns at eddies you simply can't see ahead of time. The biggest rock will easily overturn all kinds of river craft; I swamped a canoe here once myself and lost my glasses and a favorite hat. The rock will also wrap canoes around it quite nicely. If this happens, you're in for a swim of several miles until you can get out of the canyon. At high water, you're really taking your life in your own hands. The Rockslide is the main reason I recommend doing this trip only with a guide. I cannot emphasize this enough.

Day Four
Morning
- ✔ **Down Old Maverick Road**
- ✔ **Up Ross Maxwell Drive**
- ✔ **Lunch at Castolon**

Afternoon
- ✔ **Window Trail** *(Top Hike 4)*
- ✔ **Cookout or Dinner at Chisos Mountain Lodge**
- ✔ **Ranger Talk**

Day Five

Morning
- ✔ **Grapevine Hills** *(Top Hike 5)*

Afternoon
- ✔ **Lost Mine Peak Trail** *(Top Hike 1)*
- ✔ **Cookout or Dinner at Chisos Mountain Lodge**
- ✔ **Ranger Talk**

BIG BEND NATIONAL PARK 4-WHEEL DRIVE OPTION

Day One
- ✔ **Orientation at Panther Junction HQ.**
- ✔ **Down Old Maverick Road**
- ✔ **Terlingua Abaja.** ★★ A marked spur road leads to Terlingua Abaja from the Old Maverick Road, 2 miles north of the Santa Elena Canyon Overlook. A primitive campground and parking lot is at the end of the road, and the trail leads up a small cliff into a series of ruins with a view of the mouth of Santa Elena Canyon that can be spectacular depending on the light, usually best in the early morning. If you walk across Terlingua Creek, you'll find even more ruins and several graves from this old farming community. Respect the area: No collecting, climbing on ruins or tampering with grave sites. The tower and cable strung across the creek are parts of an International Boundary Commission gauging station, recording the creek's water flow into the Río Grande. According to reports from early in this century, cottonwood trees were very thick in this area. Only a few remain. (See Appendix on Place Names for the difference between Terlingua Abaja, Terlingua Ghost Town and Terlingua Ranch.)
- ✔ **Up Ross Maxwell Drive.**
- ✔ **Santa Elena Canyon Trail** *(Top Hike 8)*
- ✔ **Burro Mesa Pour-off**
- ✔ **Castolon**
- ✔ **Ruins**
- ✔ **Cookout or Dinner at Chisos Mountain Lodge**
- ✔ **Ranger Talk**

Day Two

✔ **Old Ore Road.** ★★ This, along with the River Road, noted below, are bona fide four-wheel drive, high-clearance vehicle dirt roads. They both start off passable enough, but gradually turn into terrible routes that will test you and your car. You'll need lots of water for both.

The Old Ore Road isn't traveled much. This was the route that wagons took hauling lead and zinc from Río Grande Village and Boquillas to Marathon. Fluorspar is found in abundance along this area of the Río Grande and is used in making hydrofluoric acid and in the production of enamel, glass, and steel. You can usually find some for sale at gift shops in Ojinaga and the Terlingua Trading Company in the Ghost Town.

The best way to take the Old Ore Road is north to south, giving you sweeping vistas across Tornillo Creek of the Chisos Mountains. The early morning light here makes for great photographs when skies are clear.

The road is mostly over desert, much of it unremarkable. You will, however, pass by ranch and ore terminal ruins.

✔ **Ernst Tinaja** (Top Hike 2). Off the Old Ore Road a few miles north of its junction with the main park road, Ernst Tinaja also has a primitive campground so it's a great place to spend a night and cook out under the stars.

✔ **Cookout or Dinner at Chisos Mountain Lodge**

✔ **Ranger Talk**

Day Three

Morning

✔ **Grapevine Hills** *(Top Hike 5)*

Afternoon

✔ **Lost Mine Peak Trail** *(Top Hike 1)*

✔ **Cookout or Dinner at Chisos Mountain Lodge**

✔ **Ranger Talk**

Day Four

✔ **River Road.** ★★★ A wicked road in more ways than one. It's about 50 miles long, and it will take you all day to travel it, especially if you make the detour to Glenn Spring (and you should). Please note that this road is often closed during and after wet weather and you should heed those closings absolutely.

The road follows the Río Grande sometimes, but the middle portion around Mariscal Mountain is far from the river. Along the way, you'll pass by several ruins, some occupied as recently as the 1930s, campsites, and several jeep trails to fishing camps. Also, ruins of the Mariscal Mine can be visited.

Be aware that ruins at the cinnabar mine may contain toxic levels of mercury, so you shouldn't handle any building materials. Mine shafts are now gated.

Across the river is the farming community of San Vicente.

The road offers a unique view of the Chisos Mountains. If you catch the morning light traveling east to west there are several photographic possibilities.

✔ **Glenn Spring.** ★★★ Glenn Spring Road cuts off from River Road, running along the eastern edge of the Chisos to the abandoned town of Glenn Spring that once had a large candelilla wax factory. History buffs should love this place. In 1916, on May 5 (the Cinco de Mayo holiday was probably not a coincidence), a band of Mexicans believed to be Villistas attacked the town where a small contingent of U.S. cavalry was stationed. Three American soldiers and a small boy were killed, the store looted, a couple of buildings burned, the wax factory destroyed. After the border troubles, the town was rebuilt, but it was never the same again and wasted away over the next two decades.

The spring here still flows, but all that's left of the town is an old corral and cemetery. The gravel road to the spring is steep and strewn with loose rocks. The only way out is back up that incline, so unless you have a vehicle you know will climb that return trip it's best to park above the spring and hike down.

✔ **Cookout or Dinner at Chisos Mountain Lodge**

✔ **Ranger Talk**

Day Five

Morning

✔ **Window Trail** *(Top Hike 4)*

Afternoon

✔ **Paint Gap Road.** ★★ This is a true desert road, about 4 miles long, and gets exceptionally rough as it passes through the actual gap in the hills. It's in the same general area as the Grapevine Hills Road and passes through similar scenery. Once inside the gap you might notice that some areas of the cliffs have been whitewashed. What you're seeing is actually turkey vulture droppings and such a heavy concentration means you're around a vulture roost of significant size. Because vultures feed only on dead animals, don't worry about them too much as long as your car doesn't break down.

The ruins you see at the end of the road are all that remains of an old ranch. When you get out of your vehicle to look around, you might marvel that anyone could ranch with any success out here. If you look around a little, you'll discover a spring (look for the ferns hanging from the canyon wall).

When you return to the main, paved road you'll see a great view of the Chisos Mountains.

✔ **Dinner at the Starlight in Terlingua**

BIG BEND RANCH STATE PARK OPTION

Day One
  ✔ **Drive Ranch Road 2810 from Marfa to Chinati Hot Springs**
  ✔ **Stay at Chinati Hot Springs**
Day Two
Morning
  ✔ **Fort Leaton State Historic Site**
  ✔ **Lunch at The Patio in Presidio**
Afternoon
  ✔ **Drive Park Road to Solitario Viewpoint.** ★★★ This long, gravel road is interesting in itself. Keep an eye out for odd rock formations and one area, known as Las Cuevas that has dozens of small caves covering the nearby cliff walls. If you're planning on camping out, you'll find about a dozen marked sites along this road. Along the roadside, you'll also see dozens of new signs pointing out interesting historical or geological features, so stop and check them all out.

Stop at the **Sauceda Visitors Center** to get oriented and pick up literature and maps on the park, then continue east to the Solitario.

The Solitario dome is about 10 miles in diameter and the viewpoint will give you a great view of this collapsed volcano, one of the largest and most symmetrical molten-rock domes in the world. The only better view you can get is from a plane. The highest point in the folded walls below you is 5,120 feet at Fresno Peak. The oldest rocks here are about 520 million years old and were once the floor of a vast ocean that covered all of Big Bend in ancient history.

✔ **Camp Out or Stay at La Sauceda.**

Day Three

✔ **Encino Loop Trail.** ★★ This is actually a hike or bike route. If you brought your mountain bikes, this is the place to take them out. If you decided to hike, though, it's an easy walk but it does cover 8.5 miles. It's a fairly level trail all the way, and provides you with a real feel for what it must have been like out here when this was a working cattle ranch.

Before you head out, though, get a trail map from the Visitors Center.

✔ **Oso Loop.** ★★★ This is actually a four-wheel drive road, so if you have that type of vehicle you're in great shape. However, this loop is also a very interesting trail for bikes, even though it's pretty strenuous.

The 6-mile loop climbs through the desert to higher elevations with nice scenic views of mountains and volcanic dikes, plants and animal life.

Again, get a trail map from the Visitors Center before you head out. And remember to close all the gates behind you.

✔ **Camp Out or Stay at La Sauceda**

Day Four

✔ **Explore Las Cuevas**

✔ **Ojito Adentro** *(Top Hike 10)*

✔ **Cinco Tinajas** *(Top Hike 9)*

✔ **Camp Out or Stay at La Sauceda**

Day Five

✔ **Farm Road 170**

✔ **Big Hill**

✔ **Contrabando Movie Set**

✔ **Closed Canyon** *(Top Hike 7)*

✔ **Dinner at Lajitas**

WHAT TO DO IN TEN DAYS
BIG BEND NATIONAL PARK

Day One
Morning
- ✔ Farm Road 170
- ✔ Fort Leaton State Historic Site
- ✔ Closed Canyon *(Top Hike 7)*

Afternoon
- ✔ Contrabando Movie Set
- ✔ Terlingua Ghost Town
- ✔ Dinner at the Starlight Restaurant

Day Two
- ✔ Orientation at Panther Junction HQ
- ✔ Down Old Maverick Road
- ✔ Luna's Jacal
- ✔ Terlingua Abaja
- ✔ Up Ross Maxwell Drive
- ✔ Santa Elena Canyon Trail
- ✔ Burro Mesa Pour-off
- ✔ Castolon
- ✔ Ruins
- ✔ Cookout or Dinner at Chisos Mountain Lodge
- ✔ Ranger Talk

Day Three
Morning
- ✔ Hot Springs
- ✔ Ernst Tinaja

Afternoon
- ✔ Lost Mine Peak Trail
- ✔ Cookout or Dinner at Chisos Mountain Lodge
- ✔ Ranger Talk

Days Four and Five

✔ **Santa Eleña Canyon River Raft Trip**
Day Six
Morning
  ✔ **Grapevine Hills Trail**
Afternoon
  ✔ **Study Butte**
  ✔ **Indian Head and Red Rocks.** ★★★★ This is a little-known, amazing trail that is in the national park but you must access it from Study Butte, several miles away from the main park entrance. It's a great place for a picnic, and you won't find too many people around. Go down the Indian Head Road located near the Big Bend Resort and Adventures main office. Follow this dirt road around to the left of the old dump, then when it forks again turn to your right. Pull in at an expansive parking area. Ahead of you look for a dwelling high in the cliffs. Walk down a hill to the narrow opening in the fence marking the park boundary and follow the trail. It's an easy, mostly level trail. To your right you have unobstructed scenic views of the Chisos Mountains. To your left are the red rocks that look like crusty and rusted metal. Those two reasons are enough to take this hike, but there's more. A lot more. Take your time and look closely at the rocks as you roam around and you will see ancient pictographs. Hundreds of them. Scramble around behind some of them and discover even more. I think this place is breathtaking.
  ✔ **Terlingua Ghost Town**
  ✔ **Dinner at Starlight Restaurant**
Days Seven and Eight
  ✔ **South Rim Trail** *(Top Hike 6)*
Day Nine
Morning
  ✔ **Dagger Flats**
Afternoon
  ✔ **Window Trail** *(Top Hike 4)*
  ✔ **Cookout or Dinner at Chisos Mountain Lodge**
  ✔ **Ranger Talk**

Day Ten
Morning

✔ **Chimneys Trail. ★★★** Here's a real desert walk, and if you do it in summer you're out of your mind. It's a moderately strenuous 5-mile round-trip from the Ross Maxwell Drive to the Chimneys, an eroded dike where Indian petroglyphs and pictographs can be found. Remarkably, you'll also find the remains of shelters used by goat herders and a stock tank. You can make this an all-day hike of about 7 seven miles, walking from Maxwell Drive to near Luna's Jacal on the Old Maverick Drive, but you'll need a shuttle car and you'll need to be in good shape.

Afternoon

✔ **Chisos Basin Loop. ★★** A relatively easy hike, if you stay on the right trail, this loop will give you commanding views all around the Basin and a unique perspective on The Window. The trail itself is about a mile and a half round trip, but it crosses other trails along the way—Laguna Meadow and the Pinnacles--so make certain you're on the right one or you'll wander into strenuous territory for a long way. On the Loop, you hike through much of the same flora--juniper, oak, and pine trees—that you'll find on the most robust hikes like the South Rim or Lost Mine Peak. All this dense foliage and the arroyos are places black bears and mountain lions love to hang around, so be aware of your surroundings.

✔ **Cookout or Dinner at Chisos Mountain Lodge**

✔ **Ranger Talk**

APPENDICES

Perhaps our generation will come to appreciate the Southwest as the country God remembered and saved for man's delight when he could mature enough to understand it. God armored it with thorns on the trees, stings and horns on the bugs and beasts. He fortified it with mountain ranges and trackless deserts. He filled it with such hazards as no legendary hero ever had to surmount.

— Erna Ferguson

APPENDIX A
RECOMMENDED READING

NOTE: Some of the books listed below are out of print (marked *). Although some might be a little out of date as well, they all provide valuable information to the Big Bend. Many such books may still be acquired on Web sites such as amazon.com, eBay, or craig's list.

Folklore

• *A Bowl of Red* by Frank X. Tolbert (Doubleday). Ever wonder how the chili cook-off phenomenon got its start? It's all documented here by the man who was present at the beginning in Terlingua.

• *How Come It's Called That?: Place Names in the Big Bend Country* by Virginia Duncan Madison and Hallie Crawford Stillwell (Iron Mountain Press). Stories behind all those places you're driving through by two of the area's legendary women.

• *The Legend of Fort Leaton* by Allan C. Kimball (Sun Country Publications). Historical fiction about a unique private fortress near Presidio that was partially restored and is now part of the Big Bend Ranch State Park complex.

• *Tales of the Big Bend*
• *More Tales of the Big Bend*
• *Stray Tales of the Big Bend* by Elton Miles (Texas A&M University Press). A former professor of English at Sul Ross University, Miles has drawn on his decades of experience and numerous contacts in the Big Bend area to produce the finest series of true and legendary stories you will find. Makes for first-rate evening reading while on a Big Bend trip or just the thing for that rainy day when the stories will take your imagination far, far away.

• *Tales From the Terlingua Porch* by Blair Pittman (Sun Country Publications). Collection of stories from one of the area's true characters.

Guidebooks

• *Hiker's Guide to Trails of Big Bend National Park*
• *Road Guide to Backcountry Dirt Roads of Big Bend National Park*
• *Road Guide to Paved and Improved Dirt Roads of Big Bend National Park.* Published by the Big Bend Natural History Association, these three guides are invaluable. The *Hiker's Guide* describes the most popular hikes in the park, giving distances, directions, and rating their difficulty. The *Road Guides* offer a mile-by-mile account of what you'll encounter along the park's roads.

The guides are available at most outdoor stores, many Big Bend area bookstores and gift shops, ranger stations in both the national and state parks, and from the BBNHA, P.O. Box 196, Big Bend National Park, TX 79834.

Geology/Nature

• *The Big Bend of the Rio Grande: A Guide to the Rocks, Geologic History, and*

Settlers of the Area of Big Bend National Park by Ross A. Maxwell (University of Texas Press). A comprehensive book, to the point of including separate maps in a back pocket. Full of historic photos and written by the park's first superintendent.

- *God's Country or Devil's Playground* edited by Barney Nelson (University of Texas Press). Collection of writings from the experts.
- *Mountain Islands and Desert Seas* by Frederick R. Gehlbach (Texas A&M University Press). A natural history of the Big Bend, geology told in a personal approach.
- *A Road Guide to the Geology of Big Bend National Park* by Kerri Nelson (Big Bend Natural History Association). Comprehensive and not beyond an amateur's understanding.

Hiking

- *The Complete Walker IV* by Colin Fletcher and Chip Rawlins (Knopf). Although not a Big Bend book, this is the hiking tome by which all others should be judged. Even if you're a casual walker and not a die-hard backpacker, this book will be of great help and amusement.
- *Desert Survival Skills* by David Alloway (University of Texas Press). Want to be safe while hiking across the Chihuahuan Desert? This great book will help accomplish that.

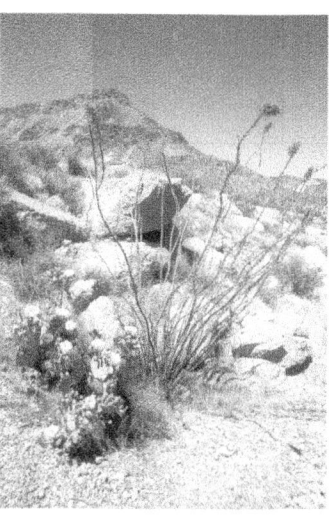

- *Hiking Big Bend* by Laurence Parent (The Globe Pequot Press). Dozens of hikes in the national park and a couple in the state park are featured along with details such as maps and distances.

History

- *Bandido* by Tony Cano and Ann Sochat (Reata Publications). Biography of Big Bend bandit Chico Cano, who was a legend in these parts.
- *Big Bend Country* by Ross A. Maxwell (Big Bend Natural History Association). Insider detail and historic photographs by the man who was there from the beginning.*
- *The Big Bend Country* by Virginia Madison (University of New Mexico Press). Written in 1955, this isn't up-to-date, but it is full of great stories of the Big Bend's past by one of its premier chroniclers.
- *The Big Bend: A History of the Last*

Frontier by Ronnie C. Tyler. A National Park Service book that is nearly exhaustive in its scope and full of historical photographs.

• *Big Bend: A Homesteader's Story* by J.O. Langford with Fred Gipson (University of Texas Press). A first-hand story of how the Langford family built and ran their desert hot springs resort.

• *The Buffalo Soldiers: A Narrative of the Negro Cavalry in the West* by William H. Leckie (University of Oklahoma Press). The famed buffalo soldiers were stationed at Fort Davis and other smaller Big Bend-area army posts. This book was the first to set off the modern interest in those black pioneers.

• *The Great Pursuit: Pershing's Expedition to Destroy Pancho Villa* by Herbert Molloy Mason, Jr. (Smithmark Publishers). Top account of the famed Punitive Expedition that determined much of Big Bend history. This is one of the only complete histories.

• *I'll Gather My Geese* by Hallie Crawford Stillwell (Texas A&M University Press). A great firsthand account of life in Big Bend told by a true legend. Stillwell was a wife, mother, schoolteacher, ranch manager, and justice of the peace, and died just short of her 100th birthday. A museum dedicated to her remarkable life is down Ranch Road 2627 just east of the park.

• *Little Known History of the Texas Big Bend* by Glenn Justice (Rim Rock Press). A recent look at the history of the area from the days of Cabeza de Vaca to the days of Pancho Villa using mostly primary sources.

• *A Most Singular Country: A History of Occupation in the Big Bend* by Arthur R. Gomez (Brigham Young University/Big Bend National Park). Perhaps this book's title should more properly be a history of European occupation in the Big Bend, but that aside, it's a comprehensive account of those who have passed through and those who have stayed in the most inhospitable of areas.

• *The Old Army in Texas* by Thomas T. Smith (Texas State Historical Association). A research guide to the U.S. Army in 19th century Texas.

• *Quicksilver: Terlingua and the Chisos Mining Company* by Kenneth Baxter Ragsdale (Texas A&M University Press). Everything you could possibly want to know about Howard E. Perry's cinnabar mine and mining in general in the Big Bend.

• *Seeds of Man* by Woody Guthrie (Bison Books). An obscure book filled with Guthrie's adventures in the Big Bend when he was a young man, showing ranch and town life and offering a tantalizing report of a lost gold mine. Son Arlo told me once that members of his family still occasionally search for that gold.

• *Shod With Iron* by C.M. "Buck" Newsome (Anchor Publishing). An intimate and often hilarious look at life along the U.S.-Mexico border by an old Border Patrol agent. Has one of the best opening paragraphs of any book, and if you can read it without wanting to read the rest of the book you have no sense of humor or curiosity.

• *Standing in the Gap* by Loyd M. Uglow (Texas Christian University Press). The story of the U.S. Army on the Texas frontier.

• *Texas Indian Trails* by Daniel J. Gelo and Wayne J. Pate (Republic of Texas Press).

Unusual book that is part travel guide, part folklore, and part history.

• *Texas and the Mexican Revolution* by Don M. Coerver and Linda B. Hall (Trinity Press). The Mexican Revolution of the early 1900s shaped much of the culture and attitude of the border along the Río Grande.

• *Unlikely Warriors: Benjamin Grierson and His Family* by William H. Leckie and Shirley A. Leckie (University of Oklahoma Press). Here's a close look at what it was like to serve in the army on the Texas frontier during the Indian Wars. Grierson was a Civil War hero and one of the most prominent commanders of Fort Davis.

• *Wings Over the Mexican Border* by Kenneth Baxter Ragsdale (University of Texas Press). Military aviation got its start in the Big Bend as the fledgling Army Air Corps and its fragile biplanes stalked the desert in search of Pancho Villa and other desperadoes. This is that story.

Historical Novel

• *Rainbows Wait For Rain* by Allan C. Kimball (Sun Country Publications). OK, this is a shameless plug for the book that collects my Western trilogy (*Calamity Creek, Woman Hollering Creek* and *Second Coffee Creek*) into one volume. This is one of the few Westerns set in the heart of the Texas Big Bend country in the 1880s. Visit the Website at www.rainbowswaitforrain.com to get more information.

Photography

• *Big Bend National Park* by Joe Nick Patoski and Laurence Parent (University of Texas Press). Excellent introduction to the park by a writer who knows it intimately and a photographer who can capture its essence.

• *Big Bend National Park Impressions* by Steve Guynes and Richard Reynolds (Far Country Press). Color photographs so vivid you'll wish you were there. Right now.

• *Big Bend Pictures* by James Evans (University of Texas Press). Black and white photography, with an emphasis on people, by one of the best picture-takers in the area.

• *Big Bend: Three Steps to the Sky* by Frank Deckert (Big Bend Natural History Association). Great color photographs of Big Bend National Park and a good cursory introduction to the area.

• *Chronicles of the Big Bend: A Photographic Memoir of Life on the Border* by W.D. Smithers (Madrona Press). This book could also easily be included under the history section. It's one of the best of both. Smithers was in the right place at the right time, documenting people and events in the Big Bend at the turn of the last century. Excellent.

• *Desert Sanctuaries* by Wyman Meinzer and David Alloway (Texas Tech University Press). Explore Big Bend Ranch State Park and the Chinati Mountains in color photos.

• *Land of the Desert Sun* by D. Gentry Steele (Texas A&M University Press). Black and white photos of the Big Bend.

• *The Terlingua Area* by Dimitri Gerasimou (DeGe-Verlag). Color portraits of the landscape, ruins, and colorful folks that have made Terlingua what it is.

• *Texas West of the Pecos* by Jim Bones, Jr. (Texas A&M University Press). Fine color photographs by an artist who is synonymous with Big Bend.

• *Where Rainbows Wait For Rain* by Richard Fenker Jr. and Sandra Lynn (Tangram Press). Ethereal, almost mystic, black-and-white photographs by Fenker and evocative poetry by Lynn. An effective combination.

Plants

• *Naturalist's Big Bend* by Roland H. Wauer (Texas A&M University Press). First-rate introduction to all the trees, plants, wildflowers and wildlife you'll see in the area.

• *Wildflowers of the Big Bend Country, Texas* by Barton H. Warnock (Sul Ross State University). This is an indispensable guide to area plants, designed for quick references. Full of great color photography by Peter Koch.*

APPENDIX B
CAR CAMPING CHECK LIST

Here's a handy ✔ checklist to make sure you have everything you may need before you head out for Big Bend.

- ❏ Alternator and fan belts (if going off paved roads)
- ❏ Books
- ❏ Chairs
- ❏ Charcoal (if cooking out)
- ❏ Clothing
- ❏ Compass/GPS
- ❏ Cooler
- ❏ Cooking utensils (if cooking out)
- ❏ Cookstove (if cooking out)
- ❏ Dishwashing soap (if cooking out)
- ❏ Duct tape
- ❏ First aid kit
- ❏ Flashlight
- ❏ Food
- ❏ Hats
- ❏ Hiking boots
- ❏ Jumper cables
- ❏ Maps
- ❏ Paper towels
- ❏ Pots/pans (if cooking out)
- ❏ Radiator hose (if going off paved roads)
- ❏ River shoes (if taking river trip)
- ❏ Sleeping bags (if camping)
- ❏ Shovel (short handle)
- ❏ Soap (if camping)

- ❏ Sunglasses
- ❏ Sunscreen
- ❏ Swim suits
- ❏ Tent (if camping)
- ❏ Toilet articles
- ❏ Tool kit (if going off paved roads)
- ❏ Trash bags
- ❏ Water bottles/canteens
- ❏ Water jug (5 gallon)

APPENDIX C
BIG BEND NAMES

Here is a list of some of the common names found in the Big Bend, their meaning and pronunciation.

Alpine — [Al-pine] You might not think anyplace in a desert should be called Alpine, but this city sits at 4,481 feet elevation, surrounded by taller peaks. The city has a population of about 6,000 and is home to Sul Ross University and the Museum of the Big Bend.

Boquillas — [Bow-kee-ahs] Means little mouths, named for the narrow mouth of the canyon that bears the name. Also the name of a small Mexican village near the canyon.

Cañon Obscuro — [Canyon Ob-skurr-oh] Most people call this place Closed Canyon. Either version makes sense. As you walk in, the canyon's steep walls create pockets of darkness, hence the "obscuro." And as you continue walking, the canyon gets narrower and narrower, until you can travel no further, hence the "closed."

Candelilla — [can-duh-lee-ah] This is a spindly little plant you see just about everywhere you walk in Big Bend. For many years, people here harvested candelilla and you can still find old candelilla camps scattered in the backcountry. You can recognize them because they are usually located near a source of water and one or more 50-gallon steel drums are rusted out nearby. They would boil the candelilla with chemicals to extract wax from the plant. The wax was used in car polish, shoe polish and chewing gum. Still is. Check the ingredients on that pack of Chiclets.

Casa Grande — [Cah-sa Gran-day] Spanish for big house, and when you see it you'll know why it's called that. Casa Grande is a highly visible landmark, often photographed framed in the Window from the desert side or from along the Window Trail. It's tempting to want to climb it, but the National Park Service won't allow it because the rocks are too loose for stable footing. You can get near the top by following Lost Mine Peak Trail, however.

Castolon — [Cas-toe-loan] The most common explanation given for the name of this now abandoned farming community on the Ross Maxwell Drive is that it is a variation on Cerro Castellan, the landmark mountain that looms over the town. Cerro Castellan, in turn, is a corruption of words meaning great castle. But some say Castolon was a corruption of the name Castulo, a pioneer who lived here.

Chihuahua — [Chee-wa-wa] Probably from the Aztec word "xicuauhua," meaning a very dry place. The word applies to the vast Chihuahuan Desert, the Mexican state of Chihuahua that borders part of Big Bend, the city of Chihuahua, the Chihuahuan Trail, and, of course, that little yappin' dog.

• The Chihuahuan Desert is a high desert that sweeps across much of southwest Texas and southeast New Mexico and central northern Mexico with average elevations in the 3,500 feet to 4,200 feet range. The desert is trapped by the Rocky Mountains, Sierra Madre Oriental and Sierra Madre Occidental ranges.

• Chihuahua — Mexico's largest state of about 95,000 square miles and more than 2 million people borders Big Bend from about the midpoint of Big Bend National Park westward to the New Mexico/Arizona state lines. Most of the state has mountains, canyons, rivers and vistas rivaling or better than the Big Bend but it is very inaccessible for a casual traveler.

• Ciudad Chihuahua — This state capital, originally called San Felipe del Real de Chihuahua, was settled in the late 1500s at the confluence of the Chuviscar and Sacramento rivers, and has a rich history. The Battle of Sacramento, fought near here, was a major U.S. victory in the Mexican War.

The city is about 140 miles southwest of Presidio down Mexico Highway 16. With a population of more than 500,000, Chihuahua boasts a university and is now the center of a cattle-raising area. The San Francisco church is one of the best-known examples of 18th century architecture in Mexico and is very photogenic. The justly famous Copper Canyon train trip begins here, traveling through primitive Tarahumara Indian country with a canyon deeper than the U.S. Grand Canyon, and ending at Los Mochis on the Gulf of California.

• The Chihuahua Trail — In the frontier days of the middle 1800s, this trail for pioneers and traders went from Ciudad Chihuahua to San Antonio de Bexar via the Presidio area. You can follow portions of it through very rugged desert along Ranch Road 169 south of Marfa off U.S. 67.

• Chihuahuan dogs — Although named for the state where the breed was first noticed, you'll be hard-pressed to find any Chihuahuas in Chihuahua now. Remarkably, they are descended from the techichi, a mute dog kept by the Toltecs. You either love 'em or you hate 'em.

Chisos — [Chee-zos] Much disagreement surrounds this most vivid of mountain range names. Some say the word is a corruption of "chivos," a slang word for goats, because much goat herding has gone on in the area over the centuries. Some say the name derives from the word "chishi," a common word meaning people of the forest that was used to refer to Apaches by other Southwestern tribes. Others say the word means ghost, and legends of people seeing the ghost of Chief Alsate abound. Still others insist the name stems from "hechizos," meaning enchantment. When you see the mountains rise from early morning mists, you can decide which version you like.

Cholla — [choy-ah] A hardy little desert cactus with chubby, spiked limbs. It's seen everywhere in Big Bend, and often you will find cactus wrens building their nest in its limbs.

Ernst — Max A. Ernst was a pioneer settler in the Big Bend, operating his Big Tinaja Store and post office in the town of La Noria. Ernst Tinaja, Ernst Basin, Ernst Gap, Ernst Valley and the Ernst geological formations are named for him. He was shot in 1908 at Ernst Gap, near where the tunnel at Tornillo Creek now is. He died the next day without telling anyone who had shot him. His killer was never found.

Fort Davis — This national historic site is one of the best-restored frontier forts in the nation. It was founded in 1854 and named for Secretary of War Jefferson Davis. Davis would gain some fame in the Big Bend for his camel experiment. Believing that the U.S. Army would do better with camels as cavalry mounts, Davis conducted studies in the area that proved him correct in the late 1850s. The Civil War interrupted all that, but abandoned camels were being seen in the area for a couple of decades. Davis went on to greater notoriety as president of the Confederacy. Union forces abandoned the fort to Confederates during the war, but rebuilt and expanded it after the war. Why the U.S. Army never bothered to change the name of a fort named for the leader of the recently rebellious states is a wonderment.

Fort Leaton — [Fort Lee-tun] Ben Leaton was a scalp hunter in Mexico who fought in the Mexican War and later married a local woman who owned property where Alamito Creek flows into the Rio Grande. They built a private fortress that covered an entire acre, trading between Ciudad Chihuahua and San Antonio. After a bloody history, the fort passed into the hands of Leaton's partner, John Burgess, who was later murdered by William Leaton, Ben Leaton's son. The Burgess family is buried at the fort. The Texas Parks & Wildlife Department has done an admirable job of restoring the old place. See the Recommended Readings appendix for a book on Fort Leaton.

Jacal — [ha-call] Spanish for shack. Usually made of adobe or rock or a combination of the two, you'll see a lot of them in Big Bend, some in ruins but some still inhabited.

Kiva — [kee-va] A kiva is a ceremonial pit house dug into the ground where prehistoric Southwestern Indians socialized and worshipped. The La Kiva bar and restaurant near Terlingua — also built under ground — serves a similar purpose for modern folks today.

Lajitas — [Lah-hee-tas] The word means little flag stones, which you'll find all around this famous ford across the Río Grande. This was the site of one of the main fords used by Comanches when they raided into Mexico. The Mexican town on the south side of the river is usually refereed to as Paso Lajitas or Little Lajitas to differentiate it from the

American resort on the north bank. Be aware that the Office of Homeland Security has closed this crossing and you may be fined heavily if caught returning. The ford here is a common put-in for river trips through Santa Eleña Canyon and sometime take-out point after running Colorado Canyon. Rafts are a common sight here early in the morning, especially weekends.

La Noria — [La Nor-ee-ah] The well. A small town, now abandoned, along the Old Ore Road and near Ernst Tinaja.

Lechuguilla — [Lech-oo-gee-ah] You'll see this stuff all over Big Bend and it is, in fact, an indicator plant of the Chihuahuan Desert. That means if you see the plant, you know you're in that particular desert since it doesn't commonly grow in any of the others. It looks kind of like an anemic agave, to which it is related. Its short, pointed leaves are vicious. The tips of the spikes are so sharp, Indians would use them as built-in needles and thread, breaking off the tips and pulling out a connected fiber from the spike.

Marathon — [Mare-eh-thun] Named for the famed ancient city in Greece, but pronounced differently. The city of about 800 is on U.S. Highway 90 about 20 miles east of Alpine, and it's home to the historic Gage Hotel. Traveling south on U.S. Highway 385 will take you to Ranch Road 2627, which leads to Stillwell, home of Big Bend legend Hallie Stillwell and the Hallie Hall of Fame. A store and RV park are adjacent to the museum. Further on that dirt road is the Black Gap Wildlife Preserve and, at the Río Grande, a relatively new take-out point for paddlers who have finished running Boquillas Canyon. U.S. 385 ends at the Persimmon Gap entrance to Big Bend National Park.

Mariscal — [Mar-ee-skal] The prettiest of the three Río Grande canyons within the national park, it's square in the middle, right where the river actually makes its big bend. It's also the most difficult to get to. Quicksilver mines are scattered all over. The word itself means blacksmith or marshal or a high-ranking official, and Mariscal Canyon and Mariscal Mountain were named for Albino Villa Alfelias, a famed Mexican Indian fighter.

Marfa — [Mar-fah] County seat of Presidio County with a beautiful courthouse, it has a population of about 2,500. A railroad executive's wife named the town for a minor character in Dostoevsky's novel *The Brothers Karamazov* that she happened to be reading at the time. The city has a growing reputation as an artists' community.

Maxwell — A few years back, Santa Eleña Drive was renamed Maxwell Scenic Drive in honor of Ross A. Maxwell, the first superintendent of Big Bend National Park and one of those instrumental in its establishment as a park in 1944.

Mesa de Anguila — [May-sah day Ahn-gee-lah] Some questions exist on the meaning of this name. Perhaps an early cartographer just misspelled a word and it stuck. ¿Quién sabe? "Anguila" means eel in Spanish, but if anyone's seen a real eel on this mesa within the last 50 million years they've been eating too many mescal worms. On the other hand, the Spanish for eagle is "águila" and this mesa has not only been a popular nesting place for eagles in the past, but for giant pterosaurs in the distant mists of time. The mesa forms the American side of Santa Eleña Canyon; the Sierra Ponce is on the Mexican side.

Ocotillo — [Ok-oh-tee-oh] One of the most common plants in the Big Bend, it has long spindly stalks that are covered with tiny green leaves in wetter weather and bloom with orange and red blossoms in spring.

Ojinaga — [Oh-hee-na-ga] Locals call Ojinaga "OJ," so when you hear someone ask if they're going to OJ or say they've just returned from OJ, they're not talking about getting orange juice or that football player what's-his-name. This quiet northern Mexico city of about 20,000 is in the state of Chihuahua, and Mexico 16, the main road from the border to Ciudad Chihuahua, begins here. The city was named for Gen. Manuel Ojinaga, a war hero. The area was known originally as La Junta de los Ríos because this is where the Río Conchos flows into the Río Grande. Without the Río Conchos, the Río Grande would have little if any water flowing in it through the Big Bend because the cities of Juárez, Mexico, and El Paso, Texas, capture most of the Río Grande water that comes out of New Mexico. The settlement was later known as Presidio del Norte, for the border fort that was established there. The city across the Río Grande that Americans now call Presidio was then called Spencer's Store or Rancho Spencer, after John Spencer, a scalp-hunting colleague of Ben Leaton's in Mexico and a pioneer settler in the area.

Ojo Caliente — [O-ho Cal-ee-en-tay] Spanish for Hot Springs, the place where J.O. Langford and his family maintained a health resort on the Río Grande from 1909 to 1942.

Paisano — [pie-zan-oh] Means little buddy in Spanish and, no, it doesn't refer to Gilligan but to what Americans call a roadrunner, that large bird you often see racing your car along the road. I've yet to hear one go "beep-beep."

Presidio — [Pree-sid-ee-oh] Means fort in Spanish and is named for the northern military outpost established in the area during the Spanish mission period of Mexico. The city of about 4,000 is most often known to Americans as the hottest place in the U.S., although that designation has been more recently usurped by Lajitas. See Ojinaga for details.

Prickly Pear — In Spanish: "nopal." This is the most common form of cactus seen in the Big Bend. When it blooms in the spring, it is beautiful. A sweet jelly and candy are made from those flower pods, and the flat pads, called "tuna" in Mexican, are also used as food for cattle and people. Don't try to touch one, even if you think you're being careful to grab between its larger spines. The pads are completely covered with thousands of almost invisible, flexible spines that will cause you days of grief. These small spines are called glochids. Get them out by using tweezers and a magnifying glass, or by covering them with duct tape and peeling off after a few minutes, or wait a couple of painful days for them to come out on their own.

Río Grande — [Ree-oh Gran-day] The river that forms the border between Texas and Mexico from El Paso/Juárez to Brownsville/Matamoros is known as the Río

Grande only in the U.S. In Mexico, it is known as the Río Bravo del Norte.

Santa Eleña — [Sahn-ta Eh-lain-yah] Name of the canyon, the largest in Big Bend National Park, with cliffs as high as 1,500 feet, and the Mexican town near the mouth of that canyon. It was common among early explorers and settlers to name a place for the saint on whose feast day the city was founded. In this case, Saint Helen on August 18.

Shafter — [Schaft-er] Ghost town along U.S. 67 between Marfa and Presidio. A few people still live here and occasionally there is a store or restaurant open. Named for Lt. Col. William R. Shafter, once commander of the garrison at Fort Davis, who later ran a silver mine here.

Study Butte — [Stoo-dy Byoot] You can always spot a tenderfoot by the way they mispronounce this crossroads town at the junctions of Texas 118 and Farm Road 170. It was named for a miner named Will Study. A butte, in case you failed geology class, is an isolated hill with steep sides. (Mesas have larger, flatter summits.)

Ruins of the mines that processed quicksilver between 1909 and 1969 can be seen in nearby hills.

Terlingua — [Ter-ling-gwa] "Tres lenguas" means three tongues, probably referring to the three languages (American, Mexican, Indian ... or, to be more precise, vernacular versions of English, Spanish and Athapaskan) that were common in the area. But that's just one theory. There are three places are found in Big Bend with this name.

• Terlingua Abaja [Ah-bah-ha], or Lower Terlingua, is the old farming community, now in ruins, near the mouth of Santa Eleña Canyon.

• Terlingua Ghost Town is the place most people associate with the name. It's now home to the Terlingua Trading Company gift shop, the Starlight Theatre restaurant, and the La Posada Milagro guest quarters and café. It's also home to the old Perry Mansion, built by a mine owner for his wife who deserted him the day after she saw Big Bend.

• Terlingua Ranch is a resort off Texas 118, 17 miles north of Study Butte, with a hotel, pool, restaurant, gift shop, RV hook-ups, campsites, and an airstrip. You get there after turning east at the big sign on Texas 118, then driving another 16 miles—the last few on dirt. Those 16 miles seem a lot farther when you're surrounded by lots of nothing, but don't give up. The resort is out there.

Tinaja — [tee-nah-ha] Spanish for earthen jar, the word means a waterhole. Tinajas of all sorts, from cup size to stock-tank size, are common throughout the rocky terrain of Big Bend, and are the main source of water for much of the wildlife in the desert. Topographic maps will often note where the larger tinajas are located, but they cannot be depended upon to have water in them. And if they do, treat that water well before you drink it — you don't know who or what has been relieving itself therein.

Some of the backcountry tinajas are cut into stunningly beautiful rock.

Tornillo — [Tor-nee-oh] The creek and the flat get their name from the Spanish word for the screw bean mesquite, which grows along the course of the drainage.

Warnock — The Barton Warnock Educational Center in Lajitas is named for one of the most famous of Big Bend residents. The late Barton Warnock was a professor at

Sul Ross University and author of the indispensable Wildflowers of the Big Bend Country Texas. His family remains one of the premier families in the area.

APPENDIX D
WEB SITES

Here are some Web sites where you can get more detailed information, especially about current weather conditions, upcoming special events, maps, restaurants and lodging.

- www.bigbendrivertours.com (Big Bend River Tours)
- www.abowlofred.com (Original Tolbert Chili Championship)
- www.chili.org (Chili Appreciation Society International)
- www.chinatihotsprings.net (Chinati Hot Springs)
- www.cmcm.cc (Chisos Mining Company Motel)
- www.desertsportstx.com (Desert Sports)
- www.farflungoutdoorcenter.com (Far Flung Adventures)
- www.ghosttowntexas.com (Terlingua Trading Company and Starlight)
- www.limpiahotel.com (Limpia Hotel in Fort Davis).
- www.nps.gov/bibe (Big Bend National Park)
- www.state.gov (U.S. Department of State)
- www.terlinguacitylimits.com (Terlingua)
- www.terlinguaranch.com (Terlingua Ranch Lodge and Restaurant)
- www.tpwd.texas.gov/state-parks/big-bend-ranch (Big Bend Ranch State Park)
- www.visitbigbend.com (General information)
- www.bigbendbookstore.org (Big Bend Natural History Association)
- bigbendholidayhotel.com (Holiday Hotel and Perry Mansion in Terlingua)
- www.bigbendresortadventures.com (motor inn, RV park, gas station and café, tours and horseback rides in Study Butte)
- www.bjrvpark.com (BJ's near Terlingua)
- www.eldorado-hotel.net (El Dorado Motel and café in Terlingua)
- www.laposadamilagro.net (guest houses and coffee shop in Terlingua)
- www.ranchotopanga.com (Rancho Topanga tent camping near Lajitas)
- www.thestarlighttheatre.com (Starlight Restaurant in Terlingua).

ABOUT THE AUTHOR

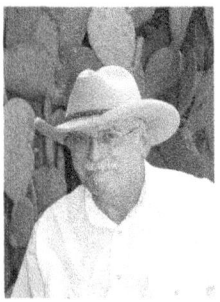

Allan C. Kimball has been visiting the Big Bend since 1969 and owns property in Lajitas and Terlingua, and has guided tours through the rugged Chihuahuan Desert.

A Navy veteran of Vietnam, Kimball is an award-winning reporter, editor and photographer who has worked at daily newspapers in Texas, including the *Pasadena Citizen*, the *Houston Post*, and the *San Antonio Express-News*. Over the years, he has interviewed several presidents, discovered clandestine government airstrips and covered stories as diverse as chili cook-offs, disastrous tornadoes, sea turtle rehabilitation and beer-drinking goats. He covered the Houston Astros and chased killer bees through Latin America.

Kimball has written two historical novels, *Rainbows Wait For Rain* and *The Legend of Fort Leaton*, was editor and co-author of *Hill Country Treasures*, and the author of travel guides *Texas Redneck Road Trips*, *Texas Museums of Discovery*, *Texas On Foot—Enjoyable Hikes and Walks*, and this *Big Bend Guide*. He is a member of the Western Writers of America.

He and his wife Madonna founded the *Hill Country Sun* magazine in 1990 and recently sold it. They live in Wimberley, Texas.